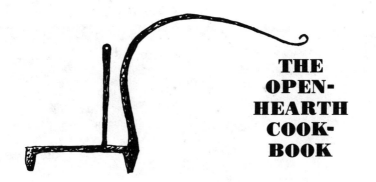

THE OPEN-HEARTH COOK-BOOK

The author's cooking hearth.

The
OPEN-HEARTH
COOKBOOK

SUZANNE GOLDENSON
WITH
DORIS SIMPSON

WITH DRAWINGS BY RICHARD F. BARTLETT

The Stephen Greene Press
BRATTLEBORO, VERMONT
LEXINGTON, MASSACHUSETTS

Produced in the United States of America.

Designed by Richard C. Bartlett

Published by The Stephen Greene Press, Fessenden Road, Brattleboro, Vermont 05301.

———————•••———————

Library of Congress Cataloging in Publication Data

Goldenson, Suzanne, 1944-
    The open hearth cookbook.

    Bibliography: p.
    Includes index.
    1. Fireplace cookery. 2. Fireplaces. I. Simpson,
Doris, 1926-   . II. Title
TX840.F5G63   641.5'8   81-20195
ISBN 0-8289-0471-5   AACR2

Contents

Preface

e first became interested in writing a book on fireplace cooking about three years ago during Thanksgiving in the Country weekend—a local house tour and fund-raiser held every year in our rural community of Sergeantsville, New Jersey. Doris Simpson and I were demonstrating our skills for the touring groups, hers being open-hearth cooking, mine, pottery. In the course of the day, we realized that we shared a common interest, collecting and using antique cooking implements. Doris is the owner and chef of a well-known local restaurant, Muirhead, and she has studied, lectured, and demonstrated extensively on the history and preparation of early American food. I, at that point, was only an inveterate collector of antiques, a fairly serious cook, and the owner of a large pre-Revolutionary walk-in cooking hearth that I was eager to put to use. Thus began our collaboration and a winter of cooking sessions that grew into this book.

While the lure and lore of old cookbooks and antique pots and other implements, and the history of how early American cooks prepared their meals at the hearth, continued to absorb and fascinate us throughout the preliminary planning and testing stages of this book, we decided to go beyond these curiosities and anachronisms and focus on how to adapt what we had learned of early cooking to the resources and tastes of the twentieth century. Although steeped in history, the following pages are intended to be a practical guide, serving to demonstrate the mystique and pleasures of fireplace cooking for readers, and bring the best of this cooking to their tables.

Although the appeal of this subject to history buffs and food historians is obvious, why, many people ask, in this age of modern conveniences, write a book for the general public about the lost, and—to some—best forgotten art of fireplace cooking? Cooking over a wood fire is bound to be more work than cooking with modern appliances. A fire is surely not as reliable or predictable a source of heat as electricity and gas, and the resulting food, it is commonly feared, is likely to be improperly cooked and unimaginably strange-tasting.

Many answers spring to our minds when these questions are raised. Most important, we insist, is that food cooked in a fireplace tastes marvelous, *better* than food cooked in most conventional ways today—the charcoal barbecue included. And with a few minor exceptions—large cakes, soufflés, and other delicate confections—most anything one could desire to eat can be easily prepared in a fireplace. Fireplace cooking is also not difficult, and will require surprisingly few new pieces of cooking gear and few new skills of the would-be open-hearth cook. Also, as a word of encouragement, while the process of cooking over a wood fire seems alien to most modern Americans (especially those who have never camped), it is the common method, today, in many other parts of the world. Pierre Franey, one of the best-known food writers and cooks today, who grew up in a provincial part of France, commented in *Craig Claiborne's Favorites From the New York Times*, published in 1975 by the New York Times Book Co., that: "I was twelve years old before I knew people cooked in any other way."

Fireplace cooking should also be attractive in light of the growing concern and interest in energy conservation in America. As of 1978, there were 25 million fireplaces and woodburning stoves in the United States, with sales up 30 percent since the beginning of the energy crisis marked by the Arab oil embargo in 1973.* In light of this trend of wood replacing fossil fuels for heating homes, the concept of using this fuel for cooking while it warms you is likely to be an idea of more than passing merit. The vision of a pot of soup simmering at your hearth as you relax in a nearby armchair reading the Sunday paper is not only an inviting one, but a practical one, too. Certainly it is a more attractive and convenient notion, than that of a pot of stew bubbling away on the top of your oil burner!

Granted, in all honesty, if pressed, we'd have to admit that fireplace cooking has its limitations. Cooking in a fireplace does involve more work than meal preparation with modern appliances. But this is primarily because most fireplaces today are not installed in the kitchen of the house where all of the cooking paraphernalia and ingredients are stored. With careful planning, the inconvenience of trips back and forth for mixing bowls, wooden spoons, salt and pepper, and other supplies, can be kept to a minimum in a fireplace cooking session. Fireplace cooking may also seem awkward at first in other ways; and temperature control, especially, may take a little practice. We hope the pointers that follow will take most of the bugs and potential failures out of these areas for you. Fireplace cooking is also a seasonal activity, not one, except in an emergency, that one would care to pursue in July. And cooking dinner for thirty in a fireplace, however well appointed, is not a realistic idea.

Statistics from the Fireplace Institute of America

But, we have found, the fun of fireplace cooking more than compensates for these drawbacks. Family and friends really seem to enjoy the experience and flavor of dinner cooked at the fireplace. And even men who would not be found within miles of their own kitchens have been seen lending a helping hand around our hearth. Add to this the practical appeal of energy conservation, and fireplace cooking emerges as an idea, to re-coin the phrase, whose time has "re-arrived."

Before we lead you step by step through the how-tos of fireplace cooking, we would like to acknowledge our indebtedness to many early American cooks who preceded us, for without them we could not have written this book. Not only did they give us hints and clues in their recipes as to how they cooked in their fireplaces, they also gave us the courage to try many cooking techniques we never would have thought could be easily performed at the hearth. For, if baking cakes in a Dutch oven was a frequent task for the early American housewife, her twentieth-century counterparts were not to be outdone. Although we consulted many old cookbooks, we are especially grateful to the following authors: Eliza Leslie, *Directions for Cookery in its Various Branches* (1848); Hannah Glasse, *The Art of Cookery Made Plain and Easy* (1796); Amelia Simmons (author of the first wholly American cookbook), *American Cookery* (1796); Susannah Carter, *The Frugal Colonial Housewife* (1772); and Mary Randolph, *The Virginia Housewife* (1855).

We would also like to thank my husband, Dan, and Barbara Morrison who read and commented on much of the material in its preliminary stages; both our families, who sampled and provided helpful criticism of the fireplace fare (the cornmeal biscuits with cracklings included in Chapter 8 were my seven-year-old son, Andy's, favorite); Rosalie Santosuosso for typing the completed manuscript; and especially my two helpers, Violet Veseulko and Dorothy Jackson, who provided substitute mothering for my two children so that I could have the time and the peace of mind to write.

Stockton, New Jersey   —Suzanne Goldenson
June 1981

To: Beverly Jones, who introduced us
and to
"Thanksgiving In the Country,"
which provided the inspiration

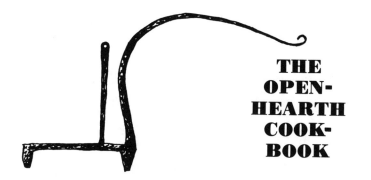

THE
OPEN-
HEARTH
COOK-
BOOK

Fireplace in the 1840 kitchen at Indian Dormitory, Mackinac Island, Michigan.

Getting Started: The Fireplace, an Inventory of Its Cooking Implements and Their Care

The Cooking Hearth

or nearly two hundred years be-
fore the first cookstoves came into use in the early 1800's, American cooks
prepared all their meals in the fireplace. In the earliest New England settle-
ments, these first cooking fireplaces were nothing more than crude open
circular hearths placed in the center of a one-room dwelling. A hole overhead
in the thatched roof permitted smoke to escape. Later, the design of these
fireplaces was improved by bringing the chimney down from the roof to form a
hood over the fire to direct the smoke upwards and out. To the hood, sides
were then added that enclosed the chimney on three sides, creating the
precursor of the modern fireplace. In these early fireplaces, the hearth
(fireplace floor) was usually made of field stones, irregularly patched together
with mud. The chimneys were built of "catted" logs (logs bonded with plaster,
sometimes called "cat" or clay) and lined with clay. They were very flamma-
ble, and because of frequent fires, the use of these materials in fireplace
construction was quickly banned. The logs and mud were then replaced by
more substantial and durable materials: stone (usually quarried granite) and
bricks held together by mortar made from natural lime deposits or pulverized
seashells. From these basic materials the first real fireplaces as we know them
today were constructed, and many of them are still standing.

The fireplace, from this point on, underwent many changes in design during
its reign as sole source of warmth and cooking heat in American homes. In
some early American dwellings, the first fireplaces were located off a central
chimney in the middle of the house with outlets in each of the rooms. This
arrangement may have become popular to avoid taxes, since a chimney tax
levied on homeowners was based on the number of chimneys in a house, and
not on the number of fireplaces it contained. But a more common location for
the fireplace was against an outside wall. This was especially true of the
kitchen fireplace.

The kitchen was the heart of the colonial home, and its fireplace reflected this. It was enormous when compared with fireplaces installed in homes today, usually at least eight, and sometimes as much as ten feet wide. It was deep as well, often accommodating a settle bench on an inside wall where family members huddled to keep warm on freezing winter evenings. These first cavernous fireplaces had no dampers. Their jambs (side walls) and back walls were built perpendicular to one another, giving the fireplace opening a boxy shape hearkening back to the design of European fireplaces of medieval times.

In the homes of more affluent families, these fireplaces frequently had a brick bake oven built into the back wall of the fireplace, either to the right or to the left of the smoke channel. The earliest of these bake ovens shared the central flue with the main fireplace. To heat them, a fire was built directly on the oven floor; the oven door was kept open to provide oxygen and to allow the smoke to escape up the central chimney flue. Later, bake ovens were improved upon by the addition of a completely separate flue, or one that fed into the main chimney flue. These modifications permitted preheating the oven with its door closed. This was a design change that not only speeded up the preheating process by cutting down on heat loss from the oven, but which also cut down on the consumption of firewood, a commodity which became scarce as time went on in the more densely populated regions. These fireplace ovens were widely

Stone, wattle, and daub fireplace, Plimoth Plantation, Plymouth, Mass-achusetts, circa 1627.

called beehive ovens since their baking chambers, which extended behind or alongside the fireplace, were dome-shaped, like a bee's nest.

The lintel or mantel support on the first cooking hearths was generally a hefty wooden beam, but sometimes granite was used. These supports did not become decorative, or even intentionally useful, elements in fireplace construction until a later period. That some of these supports protruded slightly and became used as a shelf to hold plates and other household items seems at first to have been incidental. These first cooking fireplaces were also frequently whitewashed to improve their reflecting abilities and to make them more attractive. Because of their immense proportions, and because the cook had to step into the fireplace opening to use her bake oven or to warm up on the settle bench, they have become known as walk-in fireplaces.

As craftsmen and homeowners became more skilled and experienced, fireplace construction in America improved. By the mid-eighteenth century, the bake oven was located on a front side wall of the fireplace, and its door opened into the room, instead of into the fireplace opening. Now, an ash pit was often added beneath the oven, or a chute might connect the bake oven's floor to the fireplace hearth. These features simplified the cook's job of cleaning out the ashes and remains of the fire from the oven to ready it for baking. The pit also served as a convenient storage area for ashes, which were used in making soap. Now, to preheat, load or unload her oven, the cook did not have to enter the fireplace or reach over its flames—a much safer arrangement than formerly.

With the removal of the bake oven from the brick wall of the fireplace, the fireplace opening was reduced in size and modified in design. These changes improved its efficiency for heating the room as it cooked dinner. One such refinement was to curve the bricks on its back wall increasingly inward as they rose from the floor, thus directing heat back into the room instead of sending it right up the chimney. Other sophisticated design elements were added, and the proportion between the chimney height and size and the fireplace opening were studied to increase the heating abilities of the fireplace still further, and to prevent it from smoking, a problem on windy days. The men most responsible for these improvements were two Americans, one famous and the other infamous: Benjamin Franklin and Count Rumford (Sir Benjamin Thompson). Benjamin Franklin became so absorbed with the topic of reducing smoke from fireplaces that his observations led to the invention of the damper, and then of the first woodstoves. Count Rumford, a notorious Tory who had to flee this country, focused his attention solely on the fireplace. He refined its design to such a degree that he developed a model of exceptional efficiency, which was practically smokeless. Unfortunately it required considerable skill to build a Rumford fireplace. For this reason, and because his studies coincided with the introduction of the rapidly accepted woodstove, Rumford's concepts were never widely put into use.

Kitchen fireplaces also had other special modifications and features which made them particularly suitable for cooking. A central feature of the cooking

Paired fireplaces in the Moravian Tavern, Old Salem, Winston-Salem, North Carolina, circa 1784. The left one was used for baking and washing, the one on the right for cooking with a weight-driven spit.

hearth was its crane. The crane was a large iron bracket hinged to the fireplace jamb. From S hooks and trammels placed on it, the cook suspended her cooking pots over the fire. The crane's hinges allowed her to swing it like a gate, on and off the fire, to season the soup and generally attend to her cooking food without scorching her face, getting smoke in her eyes, or reaching over the fire.

But the American housewife didn't always have this convenience. Until the eighteenth century iron was scarce, and cranes were preceded in cooking fireplaces by lugpoles. The lugpole, also called a lugstick and backbar, consisted essentially of a sturdy, very green, sapling (beech and maple were preferred) which rested on the projecting inner ledges of the fireplace throat six or seven feet above the hearth. Great care was taken to replace the lugpole before it became charred, since if it broke, it might not only spill the soup or stew, but scald the cook or a child sitting before the fire. (Death or maiming by fire and scalding water took a toll of Colonial cooks second only to death in childbirth.) Because of this ever-present hazard, and because it was very difficult for the cook to lift her heavy iron pots on and off the pothooks that attached them to the lugpole, they were readily replaced with the iron crane as soon as possible.

Also with the greater availability of iron came the introduction of a proper iron door hinged to the brickwork of the beehive oven. These replaced the fitted wooden slab or bricks which were previously pushed into place or stacked to seal the oven on baking day.

In the 1800's, firebacks or fireplates also came into use. These were thick, decorative iron slabs, sometimes incorporating an allegorical or biblical motif, or a family's coat of arms. They were set into the back walls of the fireplace and protected its masonry from the intense heat of the ever-present cooking fire, which caused deterioration of the bricks and mortar. Another practical, although minor, feature of the firebacks was that they reflected some of the fire's heat back into the room.

While the standard evolution and design of most kitchen fireplaces in America followed the preceding pattern, many early cooking hearths departed from this outline. Fireplaces reflected the imagination, ethnic origins, and resourcefulness of regional masons and home craftsmen in America. One such interesting variation in fireplace design, the cooking fireplace in General Varnum's Quarters, an eighteenth-century farmhouse in Valley Forge, Pennsylvania, is an inglenook. A Welsh custom, an inglenook is a small window or opening built into the rear wall of the fireplace. It let in additional daylight and gave the cook a glimpse of the outside world, perhaps helping to relieve the tedium of the long hours spent by the fire. There were many other fireplace variations. In the Moravian Tavern, Old Salem, Winston-Salem, North Carolina, built in 1784, the kitchen contains a pair of matching arched fireplaces. One hearth was used for brick-oven baking and washing, the other for cooking. In the South, fireplaces frequently had auxiliary cooking "counters." The Hermann Grima House kitchen in New Orleans has an example of this type of fireplace construction. Cooking counters were raised brick surfaces about waist high, many times tiled, under which a fire was built. The cook placed her pots over the circular openings in the counter, called stew holes, to heat her food. Another traditional Southern practice, especially on big plantations, was to have a separate "summer" kitchen, or to locate the kitchen away from the central living areas of the house, in its own wing. Not only was this a safety measure in light of the frequency of fires, but setting the kitchen apart kept the main house cooler during the summer months, which were particularly hot in this part of the country.

Early American Cooking Implements

At the height of the fireplace cooking era, in addition to the standard fire-tending tools—shovels, pokers, tongs, and bellows—cooks had a wonderfully innovative and versatile assortment of cooking implements and pots at their disposal. Among this impressive array, which festooned the hearth, were peels, posnets, spiders, bird ovens, coffee-roasters, tilting teakettles, ember tongs, salamanders, tin kitchens, Dutch ovens, clock jacks, griddles, waffle irons, wafer irons, spits of all lengths, and kettles of all sizes.

Of course, the kitchen fireplaces in the earliest households did not display this rich variety of accessories. In the 1600's, John Winthrop wrote to his wife to bring to Massachusetts Bay to equip her kitchen only "2 or 3 skillets of several sizes, a large frying pan, a small stewing pan, and a can to boil a pudding in. . . ." This gives a striking example of how little the fireplace cook could manage to get along with. An inventory of the furnishings in an average early American kitchen of a slightly later period was equally modest. It probably would have included an iron pot, a kettle, a large frying pan, a gridiron, a skillet or two, and a supply of wooden tableware, called "treenware." The treenware usually consisted of common eating platters (trenchers), dishes, spoons, and primitive table knives, made from sharpened sticks. Even as the country prospered and became more populated, and more kitchen implements and pots became available to cooks, most homemakers still made do with a few items. And the lavishly decorated and well-appointed kitchens at many restorations open to the public today probably present an accurate picture of only the wealthier family hearths.

Despite the generally sparse appointments of most cooking fireplaces, cooks were still able to execute all of the basic cooking techniques with a surprisingly high degree of accuracy, and with remarkably tasty results. This was due in large part to the resourcefulness of the average homemaker. Using the wooden lid of her flour barrel as a cake sheet to bake bannocks or journey cake or for planking a fish was commonplace. Pots, which were designed for a particular cooking technique, were used in a variety of other ways as well. The common boiling vessel, usually filled with a simmering soup or stew, was sometimes inverted over a bread and heaped with ashes and hot coals to form a primitive oven. The sharp edge of the exceptionally long-handled frying pan was known to have doubled as a tool to scrape kernels off ears of corn, a preliminary step in making cornmeal, which replaced wheat flour as the staff of life in early America.

An Inventory of Fireplace Cooking Pots and Implements

Here is a list of the varied implements and pots available to the early American cook and the needs that they were primarily designed to fulfill. Descriptions of how they were used by a fireplace cook in the preparation of her daily meals, and how they can be adapted or duplicated for use today, are given in the following chapters on cooking techniques.

The inventory and diagrams that follow are not typical of what would be found in an average early American kitchen. They are intended instead to show all of the implements generally developed for the cooking fireplace and to illustrate their typical cooking position on the hearth. Two distinguishing characteristics of these pots and other implements is that many of them have three short legs and curved, overhead handles, called bails. These made them particularly suitable for fireplace cooking. The feet supported the pot over a bed of glowing coals when its contents were cooking on the hearth. The curved handles allowed the cook to hang the pots and other utensils from her crane, if that was the preferred cooking location.

Andirons, cooking. These differed from common andirons in that attached to their verticals was a series of hooks to support a spitted roast. The different levels of the supports (sometimes called lugs) permitted adjustment of the distance of the roast from the fire, and thus its cooking temperature. (1)

Ash shovel. A long-handled shovel with a flat, broad end, used for removing embers and ashes from the beehive oven in preparation for baking in it. Sometimes ash shovels are confused with peels, which are wooden, since they have a similar shape, and often in a pinch ash shovels doubled for these implements. Peels, however, were used expressly for transferring breads and other foodstuffs into and out of the beehive oven. When ash shovels were used as peels, their flat end was carefully cleaned first, so that no lingering ashes would get onto the food (especially foods baked without the benefit of baking pans). (2)

Bird oven. A small, reflecting sheet-iron oven with sharp hooks for impaling small song- or game birds when roasting them before the fire. (3)

Coffee roaster. A long-handled, cylindrical metal container with a pointed end for twirling coffee beans before the fire to roast them evenly. (4)

Crane. A large iron bracket, hinged to one side of the fireplace, from which the cook hung her pots over the fire. It swung to and fro like a gate, facilitating the hanging, removal, and tending of the cooking food. (5)

Dangle spit. A three-pronged hook on a chain or trammel which meat was attached to for roasting. (6)

Doughnut kettle. A small, shallow, cast iron kettle with a bail used for frying doughnuts or fritters. (7)

Dripping pan. A pan that was placed under roasting food to catch its drippings. Early examples were squarish low containers with a handle and spouts for pouring off the accumulated grease. (8)

Dutch oven. A footed, cast iron kettle with a flanged lid and a bail. Its forté was baking, which was usually carried out on the fireplace floor. But the early American cook sometimes hung this kettle from the crane, as well. (9)

Ember tongs. Scissors-like pliers used for gripping a hot ember and passing it over food to brown its top, or for lighting pipes, candles, etc. (10)

Frying pan. A shallow, flat-bottomed, long-handled pan for frying food. It sat over the coals on a specially designed trivet with a movable arm that supported its long handle. (11)

Griddle. Not all griddles were designed to hang from the crane, but most were. They were used for baking biscuits, muffins, small cakes, pancakes, and for general sautéing. Some of the hanging griddles had small feet so that they could stand independently on the hearth, as well. Other griddles,

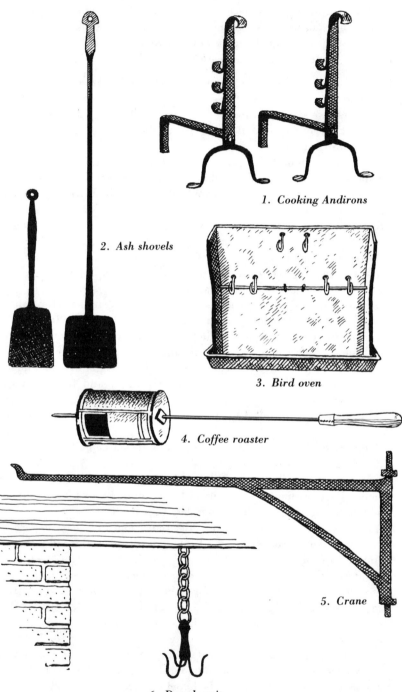

1. Cooking Andirons

2. Ash shovels

3. Bird oven

4. Coffee roaster

5. Crane

6. Dangle spit

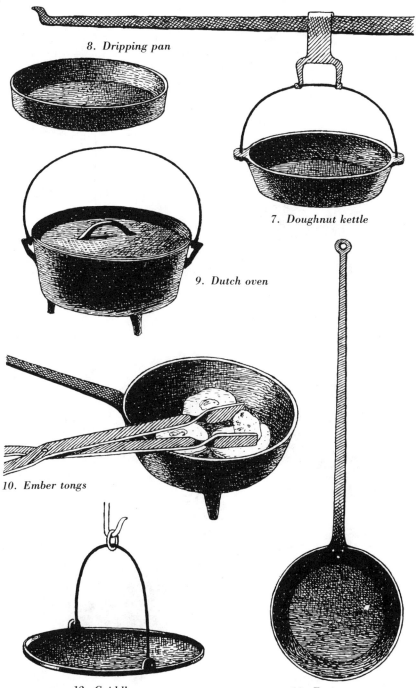

8. *Dripping pan*

7. *Doughnut kettle*

9. *Dutch oven*

10. *Ember tongs*

12. *Griddle*

11. *Frying pan*

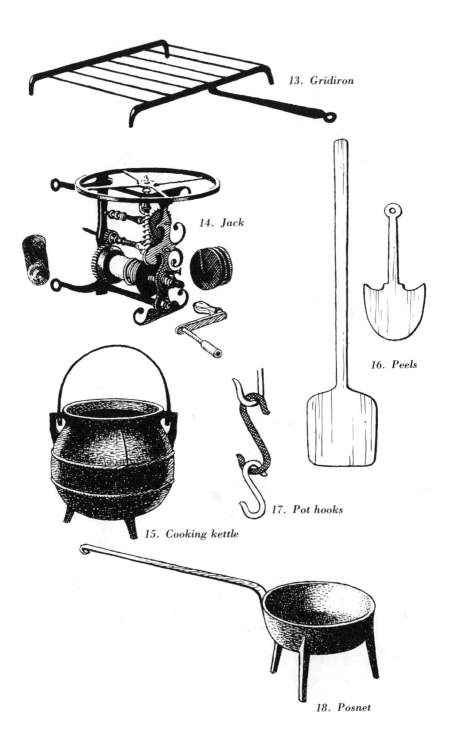

13. Gridiron

14. Jack

16. Peels

17. Pot hooks

15. Cooking kettle

18. Posnet

designed solely for use over coals on the hearth floor, usually had a single pot-like handle, rather than a bail. (12)

Gridiron. A square grill with legs and a handle used for broiling food over the coals. Gridirons also doubled as trivets for supporting pots over the glowing coals. (13)

Jacks. Mechanical devices that automatically turned the roasting food before the fire to cook it evenly. A number of different jacks were developed for fireplace use. They included: the clock jack, bottle jack, smoke jack, and steam jack. (14)

Kettle, cooking. These boiling vessels came in a variety of sizes, shapes, and materials. A common type was the rounded, cast iron model with three short legs and a bail. They are frequently referred to as gypsy or sometimes bulge kettles today. Kettles were also made of other materials, such as copper, bell metal, brass, and block tin. Not all had feet, and those that didn't usually had flat bottoms or a frame to stabilize their rounded bottoms and to raise them up over the coals for cooking purposes. (15)

Peel. A long-handled wooden shovel with a broad, flat end used for transferring foodstuffs into and out of the beehive oven. Some of the wooden peels had shorter handles. It has been speculated that these were used for removing pies, crocks of beans, and other heavier items from the oven, since the shorter handle gave the cook more control when moving these items. (16)

Pothooks. Simple, heavy wrought iron hooks for hanging implements, pots, etc. from the crane. A popular configuration for these devices was to shape them like the letter S. Hooks of this design are called S hooks. A number of S hooks could be linked together to form a chain to adjust the hanging pot's distance from the fire, and thus its cooking temperature. Pothooks in other styles were designed to fit the needs of the cook. These variations included a double-pronged version which gave pots, especially shallow ones like the doughnut kettle, extra stability when hanging from the crane. Another type of pothook acted as a lever, and allowed the cook to tilt a teakettle of hot water as it hung on the crane, and pour its contents without lifting it from the crane. (17)

Posnet. A small stewing pot or saucepan with a rounded bottom referred to in some sources as a skillet. It had a straight handle and three legs. (18)

Rotating broiler. A round, revolving wrought or cast iron grill on which the cook broiled food over the coals. It had three short legs and a straight handle. It served the same purpose as the gridiron, but its movable grilling surface gave the cook more control and more options when dealing with the broiling temperatures. (19)

Salamander. Frequently confused with the ash shovel, the true salamander was a long-handled metal device with a thick plate at one end that was preheated in the fire and used for browning off the tops of food. (20)

Skewers. Short, spear-like devices that fastened roasting meat onto the spit. The skewers were pushed into the meat through holes in the spit, and then out the other side of the roast. (21)

Spider. A shallow, black, cast iron frying pan which sat on its own splayed legs. So-called for its spider-like appearance. (22)

Spit. A long metal spear with a sharpened end that pierced the meat and supported it before the fire in a horizontal position on cooking andirons or S hooks. One end of the spit was usually articulated into a handle so that the meat could be turned easily before the fire. A variation on the standard spit was the basket spit. These had a compartment which held fragile-fleshed floods, such as fish, rather than piercing them. (23)

Teakettle. A special fireplace version had a tilter attached to its cast iron base allowing the cook to pour hot water right from the crane, so she wouldn't have to lift the heavy pot. Cast iron teakettles usually had short legs, handy when placing them over the coals or simply resting them on the hearth. More usual models, similar to those in use today, were also available in the old days. They were frequently made of brass or copper. (24)

Tin kitchen. Also called a reflector oven, it was a cylindrical tin box, open on one side, which sat in front of the fire. Its shiny surfaces reflected the fire's heat onto the sides of the food not directly facing the fire. A clever device, it came in two versions. The simpler version was for baking and had a shelf intersecting its center for placing pies, muffins, and breads to bake. A more complicated version of the tin kitchen, for roasting, came equipped with a spit instead of a shelf. In addition to the spit, it had a spout for pouring off drippings as they accumulate l, and a door in the back reflecting panel so the cook could check the progress of her roast without disturbing its position on the hearth. (25)

Toaster. Fireplace toasters came in many models. The earliest and simplest of which was a stationary wrought iron frame on three legs with a short handle. It (like the other toasters) was placed before the fire to toast its contents. "Improved" toasters featured a frame that rotated so the bread did not have to be removed to turn its other side to the fire. And in even later versions, the toaster handle was lengthened and hinged to the toast holder, so that with just a flick of the cook's wrist she could swivel the toast and expose its uncooked side to the fire. (26)

Trammel. An adjustable pothook that was used to hang cooking pots over the fire at different heights from the lugpole or crane. Common varieties were the sawtooth, chain-and-hook, and the hole-and-peg combinations. The cook could adjust and lock the trammel into different lengths, thereby changing the hanging pot's distance from the fire, and controlling the temperature of the cooking food. (27)

Trivet. A stand for supporting a footless cooking vessel, such as a frying pan, over the coals. They came in many designs, including round, and heart-shaped. Some had handles, others didn't. (28)

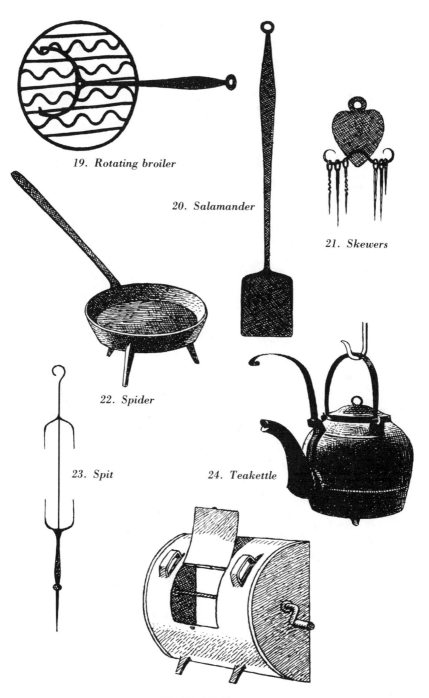

19. *Rotating broiler*

20. *Salamander*

21. *Skewers*

22. *Spider*

23. *Spit*

24. *Teakettle*

25. *Tin kitchen*

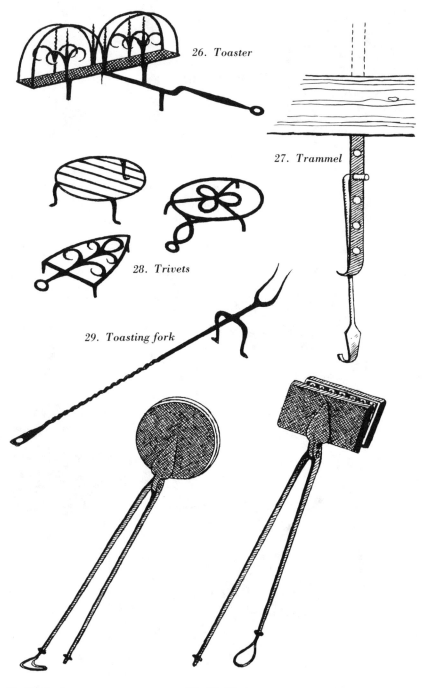

26. *Toaster*

27. *Trammel*

28. *Trivets*

29. *Toasting fork*

30. *Wafer iron*   31. *Waffle iron*

Toasting fork. A large, long-handled, two-tined fork with two small legs. It supported a tidbit of meat or bread to be cooked or toasted before the fire. The ends of the fork tines were often curved upwards so that the food would not fall off. (29)

Wafer iron. A long-handled, hinged iron for making wafers, a thin crisp cookie, at the fireplace. The wafer iron was the predecessor of the waffle iron. (30)

Waffle iron. A long-handled, hinged iron for making waffles in the fireplace. (31)

The Modern Fireplace and its Accessories for the Contemporary Open-Hearth Cook

In spite of the long list of early American cooking pots and implements just surveyed, to cook a meal in most any fireplace one needs surprisingly few accessories. Many of the implements, pots, and other materials you will need may already be on hand in your kitchen, on your workbench, or at your barbecue grill. A fireplace is, of course, a must, and although few of us will have a traditional cooking fireplace with its spacious hearth in our kitchens—or anywhere else in our homes, for that matter—this needn't be a drawback. Practically all of the cooking techniques described in this book can be executed in most any fireplace. The setting, or the furniture, rugs, and decorations that surround your fireplace, may be inhibiting factors for cooking. But fine carpeting, highly finished wood flooring, or a valuable area rug can be protected from spattering grease, straying embers, and other cooking mess, by temporarily covering them with a wool throw rug or carpet remnant for safety. The use of certain cooking implements will also help circumvent possible damage of this nature. Especially desirable for use in a pristine environment are tin kitchens, both for baking and roasting, since to use them one just pops the kitchen in front of a well-established fire. Other cooking implements and techniques that produce a minimum amount of mess and moving around of coals are described in the individual discussions of each implement's use in the technique chapters of this book.

The size of your fireplace will also be a major factor in determining how many foods one can cook in it simultaneously. Be realistic: a small fireplace may permit the preparation of only one dish at a time. This will be especially true if the hearth area is small and does not extend out into the room. A crane or a large trammel will increase the cooking capacity of a small fireplace, as a pot or two can be hung from it over the fire, while others are sitting over the coals or before the fire. So, if you intend to immerse yourself in fireplace cooking, you may want to investigate installing a crane or other pot-holders in your fireplace. Chapter 10, "Sources for Equipping Your Cooking Hearth," lists craftsmen and other outlets that can provide a crane to fit most any fireplace opening.

Besides a fireplace, and basic cooking implements, a cook will need a few fireplace tools to manipulate burning logs and coals. A shovel and a pair of wood tongs will suffice for these tasks. Bellows are nice to have, too, but not absolutely necessary. A folded magazine or newspaper will do nicely in their place for fanning the fire.

After these basics for fire-building and -tending, you will need a few implements for cooking your meal. Happily, this needn't be a long list of expensive antiques. With a few items, probably most of which are already around the house, you can cook a delicious dinner in a fireplace. Here is a list of the bare necessities needed, today, for performing the basic cooking techniques at a hearth without a crane. Precisely how they, and the antiques inventoried earlier, are used is discussed in detail in the following chapters.

A First Inventory and Its Uses for the Contemporary Fireplace Cook for Getting Started

- Butcher's twine or other stout, natural cord.
- Camp Dutch oven fitted with an interior rack (a circular wire baking rack for cooling cookies and cake layers).
- Dripping pan (any kitchen roasting pan or disposable foil baking or lasagna pan that is large enough and deep enough).
- Fire bricks, or a sturdy metal trivet with 1–2-inch-long legs.
- Grill from a barbecue (round, square, or even hinged variety).
- Kitchen pots and pans and lids of various sizes.
- Meat thermometer.
- Metal spatulas, spoons, forks, and tongs (barbecue or large kitchen cooking ones).
- Dozen new common nails, aluminum or steel, at least 1 inch long, of medium thickness, with or without heads.
- Plank of clean, hard wood.
- Pot-holders or barbecue mitts.
- Reflecting panels made out of disposable oven liners.

For roasting. Butcher's twine for trussing a roast or fowl and hanging it in front of the fire to cook; reflecting panels, improvised from two disposable oven liners, screwed or wired together to form a free-standing V, and a large roasting, or other generous-sized pan underneath to catch the drippings. These will complete the implements needed to roast a delicious entrée. For roasting a fish, a plank of wood, aluminum foil, nails, and butcher's twine are all that is required.

For toasting. A large kitchen fork.

For broiling. Aluminum foil to cover the hearth cooking area and a barbecue grill supported over the coals on two fire bricks.

For boiling, simmering, stewing, etc. A suitably sized kitchen pot with a lid adapted to fireplace use by placing it on a grill supported by two fire-bricks or a trivet to raise it above the coals.

For baking. A cast iron Dutch oven with feet, a concave lid, and a rack placed in its bottom is a must. The rack could either be a cake rack, if your oven is large enough to accommodate one, or a wire Christmas wreath form. The oven is the only item on this beginner's list of cooking tools that will cost more than a few dollars and that may involve some leg work to obtain. Dutch ovens are always available from the Boy Scouts and a number of other sources listed in Chapter 10. We should add that they are well worth the price and effort to obtain, since they are not only the best all-around implement for fireplace baking, but can be used for frying, stewing, simmering, and other cooking techniques at the hearth, as well.

For frying and sautéing. A kitchen griddle or frying pan adapted to fireplace use by placing it on a grill supported by two firebricks or a trivet.

For browning off. Tongs for passing live coals over food to brown tops.

Naturally, as you become more skilled at fireplace cooking and your appetite is whetted for more elaborate meals, you will probably want a fuller complement of fireplace cooking tools and implements. Sources for reproductions of the original antiques are listed in Chapter 10, along with suggestions on how to go about collecting the authentic antiques. But, before you begin collecting, keep in mind the spirit of improvisation ever-present in the early American household. Don't be reluctant to bring your Chinese wok or fish poacher to the hearth, for, with a trivet or fire bricks for support, they will be equally as comfortable and useful here as in your modern kitchen.

Care of Fireplace Pots and Implements

Before we turn to our discussions of the actual performance of the basic cooking techniques at the hearth, here is how to clean and care for your fireplace cooking pots—especially the iron ones.

For ordinary kitchen pots and pans adapted for fireplace cooking, the general rule is to clean and care for them as you normally would. Rubbing a bar of soap on pots' exterior surfaces before using them at the fireplace will keep them from becoming overly blackened from the carbon of the fire, and will save you a lot of extra scrubbing at clean-up time. (Iron pots, of course, will hide this discoloration.)

New iron cooking pots as well as antique ones (as soon as their rust, paint, and other residual dirt have been removed), are both "cured" and cared for in the same way. Before cooking in a new iron pot, or a professionally cleaned antique one, you must season, or "cure" it first. To do this, first scrub the pot out well with detergent and hot water, rinse thoroughly, and dry. Next, apply a coating of vegetable oil, shortening, or spray shortening, to the interior surfaces (don't forget the underside of the lid). Then heat the pot in your modern oven until the grease begins to smoke. Be sure not to let the grease burn. Remove the pot and let it cool. It is now ready for cooking. (Another way to season cast iron pots, especially the Dutch oven, is to deep-fat fry foods in them the first few times they are used.) After your cooking is completed, clean your pot, but don't overdo this step. Often, wiping it out with a damp cloth is sufficient. Never use a scouring pad on seasoned cast iron. Dry pots well. Letting the warmth of the fire accomplish this for you is an easy way. Before you put the pot away, be sure to lightly regrease it, as a buildup of these layers of grease will "sweeten" the iron and protect it from rusting, avoid discoloration, and help prevent food from sticking. Your pot is now ready for the next cooking session. It will only have to be reseasoned if you boil liquids in it, or if an unknowing helper scrubs it out too well at the conclusion of a meal.

For long-term storage of cast iron, an application of Pam, a commercial non-stick, spray shortening for cooking surfaces, is recommended. Pam does not become sticky or gummy with age or become rancid as time passes, as will some other common vegetable oils, lards, and natural greases.

The Cooking Fire

Selecting Cooking Wood

ot just any wood will suffice for building a cooking fire. And while fruit crates, old lumber, and virtually any wooden scrap material will burn, certain firewood fuels are much more desirable than others and will allow the chef to accomplish his or her cooking tasks at the hearth with the greatest degree of ease, success, and safety.

The two essential properties of the best cooking woods are that they generate an even, intense heat and that they produce a good supply of red-hot coals as combustion proceeds. The wood of trees that fall under the general classification of "hardwoods" best satisfy these two criteria.

To fully understand why the hardwoods make the best cooking fuels, we should know how the heat of the fire is used in fireplace cooking to execute the basic techniques of baking, boiling, roasting, and frying.

Early American cooks, who prepared all of their food in the fireplace (and a splendid array at that, from dainty almond cakes to roast suckling pig), usually built one central fire on their cooking hearths. From this single source, all the energy for their various cooking activities was generated. A description of these fires from the period said that they were, at their best, small, clear, and brisk. Leaping flames, or a blaze filling the entire expanse of the hearth, dramatic as these displays might have been, were of little use to the fireplace cooks of yesterday. In front of a small, controllable fire, these cooks roasted and toasted food. Suspended from a crane or trammels above the fire, their soups, puddings, and one-pot meals boiled, simmered, steamed, and stewed. And to utilize still further the fire's energy, its coals were raked or scooped up and placed on the lids and underneath specially designed fireplace pots and implements to provide the heat necessary to bake, fry, and broil simultaneously on other areas of the hearth.

From this brief glimpse of the basic fireplace cooking techniques, one can quickly see that the fire's flame rarely made contact with the food in this tradition of cooking. The most valuable qualities of the fire were that it produced a ready and plentiful supply of hot coals for performing certain cooking methods, and gave a manageable blaze for the others.

Although the special wood (hardwood) needed for a cooking fire may cost a little more and may take somewhat more trouble to locate, it's worth it! We can't emphasize strongly enough how frustrating it will be to try to duplicate the cooking techniques described in this book with wood that burns too rapidly, smokes, pops, or, what is most important, produces a few or no coals.

Wood falls into two general categories: hard and soft, with the logs of hardwood trees, as we have mentioned earlier, the preferred variety for cooking. While hardwoods are more difficult to ignite, burn less vigorously, and have a shorter flame than do the softwoods, the fires they produce are hotter, last longer, and generate more coals.

Some of the hardwoods we recommend for cooking are: ash, apple, cherry, hickory, black locust, sugar maple, and red oak. Here are a few of the special characteristics of these woods.

Ash is considered by some to be the most desirable of the hardwoods. It can be burned in a green, or unseasoned, state, as the anonymous author of the poem "Which Wood Burns Best" noted in his praise of this wood:

> But ash wood wet and ash wood dry,
> A king shall warm his slippers by.

Oak, another favored hardwood, gives off a uniform heat and short flames. It also produces a good, steady supply of glowing coals.

The wood of fruit and nut trees is among the most highly prized of the hardwoods. These woods impart a flavor and fragrance to food they cook that resembles their fruits and nuts. The smoke will also lend an aroma that will perfume your fireplace kitchen and cooking area.

By comparison, the softwoods—pine, spruce, fir, and willow, for example—are easier to ignite than hardwoods because of their high resin content. Like hardwoods, they also produce a very hot fire. But this is where their advantages for cooking end. Fires built of softwood have the tendency to pop, sending dangerous sparks and embers flying out of the hearth area, potentially harming the cook and burning the rug. These woods burn very rapidly, requiring almost constant attention in order to maintain a steady cooking temperature. Their fires generate too meager a supply of coals to permit such techniques as baking, grilling, and frying. And their resinous quality can impart a peculiar smell and taste to your food.

The only role that softwoods seem to perform successfully in the cooking fire is as an aid in fire-starting. Although we've never found it necessary, some authorities suggest that a log or two of softwood mixed in with the hardwoods will make your fire easier to ignite.

The chart in this chapter covers the relative ease of starting, splitting, and other characteristics of specific woods.

*The Relative Ratings of a Variety of Dried Hardwoods**

	Ash Red oak White oak Beech Birch Hickory Hard maple Pecan Dogwood	Soft maple Cherry Walnut	Elm Sycamore Gum	Aspen Basswood Cottonwood Yellow poplar
Relative amount of heat	High	Medium	Medium	Low
Easy to burn	Yes	Yes	Medium	Yes
Easy to split	Yes	Yes	No	Yes
Does it have heavy smoke?	No	No	Medium	Medium
Does it pop or throw sparks?	No	No	No	No
General rating and remarks	Excellent	Good	Fair *(contains too much water when green)*	Fair *(but good for kindling)*

* *Chart exerpted from Leaflet No. 559 U.S. Department of Agriculture, Forest Service:* Firewood for Your Fireplace: Selection, Purchase, Use

Buying Firewood

There are two options available for obtaining firewood: cutting and gathering it yourself in the woods, or paying someone else to do this for you. Buying your wood is obviously the easier—and the more expensive—alternative; but if your time is at a premium or if your skills and muscular abilities are unequal to the task of felling trees, it's also the most sensible. And don't forget the sawing, splitting, and hauling that the transformation of standing timber to ready-to-use firewood entails.

We prefer to buy our cooking wood. If you live in a fairly rural area, as we do, the purchasing process will usually only involve checking the classified ads in your local newspaper for the most competitive price. If you live in the city, you may have to look a little harder and drive a little farther to find competitive prices for firewood. However, price is not the sole factor to consider when choosing a wood supplier. Here are some guidelines for getting the best value out of your wood purchase.

Firewood is normally sold by the standard cord or fraction of a cord. This measurement should not be confused with either a "face cord" (sometimes called a short cord), which measures eight-by-four-by-one (or two) feet, or a long cord, which measures eight-by-four-by-four *plus* feet. The standard cord stack is eight feet long, four feet wide, and four feet high, and contains a total of 128 cubic feet.

Because the standard cord is a volume measurement, the amount of solid wood in a cord can vary greatly, depending on whether the wood pieces are straight or crooked, round or split, and large or small in diameter. These variations in shape and size can affect considerably the actual amount of wood you receive, and can account for a range of up to fifty cubic feet of wood in the supposedly standard cord. As a rule, round wood in large diameters, or split wood, neatly stacked, yields the most solid wood per cord.

Firewood is also sold by the truckload. Here, the amount of wood in a load can be estimated by the type and size of the delivery vehicle. The average pickup truck holds about two standard face cords—this is equivalent to only about 25-50 percent of the amount of wood in a standard cord. By comparison, a dump truck can hold up to four standard cords. And a large pulpwood truck with a wood rack holds anywhere from six to nine standard cords.

Another way wood is sold is by weight. If you buy wood by weight, be warned against purchasing water (which is very heavy) instead of wood. Look for the driest wood possible! Not only will you be getting more wood for your money, but you won't have to wait six to ten months while it seasons before you can burn it. Although green or unseasoned wood burns, it does so only with a lot of coaxing. It is harder to ignite than dry wood, produces less heat, and is more apt to form dangerous creosote and soot deposits in your chimney. Cracks in the ends of the logs are an indication that the wood is not green.

Here are some other factors that can affect the price of firewood.

Fruit and nut woods, because of their attractive fragrance, are in great demand, a demand that has made them the most expensive of the hardwoods. But keep in mind that they don't produce as much heat as some of the other less costly varieties, and, in practice, only a log or two of these species need be added to a fire built of the less expensive hardwoods to produce enough flavor and fragrance for an entire cooking session.

Seasoned wood costs more per cord than green wood. So, you can save yourself some money if you have a little foresight about your firewood needs. A well-ventilated, sheltered area, out-of-doors, is all you need to store your green wood. In general, wood cut in the fall or winter of one year is seasoned and ready for use by the fall of next year.

Where you live also affects the price of wood. Obviously, firewood is bound to be dearer in New York City than it is in a lumber town in Oregon, so, for city dwellers, a trip to the nearby countryside with your station wagon may be worthwhile.

Picking up, splitting, stacking, or unloading your own wood saves time and labor for the firewood dealer and can translate into dollar savings for you, as well.

The time of year when you buy your wood also affects its price. In summer, prices are usually lower than in fall and winter, when the demand for firewood increases. Miss Beecher, author of *Domestic Receipt Book, 1846,* advised the thrifty American homemaker: "Buy your wood in August or September, when it is cheapest and plenty."

Cutting Your Own

There is an old saying about wood. It warms you twice. Once when you cut it, and again when you burn it. And, with the price of firewood as high as it is and continuing to rise with the increasing popularity of woodstoves, cutting your own wood can be an attractive alternative. While it is hard, hot work, time-consuming, and frequently dangerous for the novice, it is undoubtedly the cheapest way of obtaining good cooking wood.

Here are some ideas about where to find trees for cutting for the would-be Paul Bunyan. If you are fortunate enough to own a woodlot, proper culling or thinning of your timber will not only provide you with firewood, but will improve the quality and rate of growth of your remaining trees. If you don't own a woodlot, it is often possible for a nominal fee to buy cutting and salvage rights on municipal, state, or federal lands.

Another, even easier source of firewood for the do-it-yourselfer is the local dump. Many towns prohibit open burning, and as much as 30 percent of the debris discarded in these areas may be usable wood fiber—the logs, limbs, and tops of trees toppled by storms or cleared in real estate development. This wood is often, but not always, free for the taking.

If cutting your own wood interests you, more specific information on woodlot management and splitting, seasoning, and storing firewood can be obtained from the conservation departments of most states or from your local County Extension Service agents.

Building the Cooking Fire

Building or laying a fire may on the surface appear easy, but there is a real art and even some tradition involved in constructing a fire suitable for cooking.

Historically, ways of laying a cooking fire differed in various areas of developing America. In New England, for example, the common practice was to build this fire on andirons that were modified especially for cooking. These andirons looked very much like any in use today, except for a series of hooks that protruded from their vertical columns to support the spitted meat, fish, and fowl as it roasted before the fire.

Although cooking, or spit, andirons were popular in the North, in some of the more central colonies—Berks County, Pennsylvania, specifically—the ancestry of the settlers favored a tradition of building cooking fires directly on the hearth floor. We recommend this method and describe a variation on it next. Its distinct advantage is that it requires no special or expensive equipment. While antique cooking andirons are helpful for open-hearth cooking and do add an authentic air to your fireplace, they are very rare and costly. And reproductions won't be much cheaper, since a skilled blacksmith will have to be commissioned to make them.

Here is a simple way of stacking wood for a cooking fire that the authors have found most successful, and that requires, for starters, only six good-sized pieces of split and seasoned hardwood, kindling, newspaper, matches, and a clean, clear hearth.

To lay your fire, begin by placing two of the logs on the hearth floor with their ends at right angles to, and almost touching, the rear wall of your

How to stack a double cooking fire.

fireplace. These first two logs will act as supports or "andirons" for the remaining logs. Next, lay the remaining four logs across the top of the bottom two, parallel to the back wall of the fireplace, and leave some space between them for the fire to breathe. Kindling (sticks, crumpled paper, pine cones, wood shavings, etc.) should then be placed on top of the logs and stuffed into the cracks between them, and into the low tunnel formed by the stacking configuration.

Ignite the kindling, with a makeshift torch of twisted newspaper. Next, hold the torch up the open chimney flue to encourage a healthy draft. The fire can also be fanned at this point with a bellows, magazine, or folded newspaper to ensure a strong start.

Stacking your wood in this manner leaves a natural space for the coals to accumulate in, and gives the cook easy access to them as they are needed for baking, frying, and broiling, without having to disturb the fire's design.

It is most important to maintain the fire's basic configuration when adding new logs and until all of your cooking is completed. About two hours and two generous armfuls of firewood are needed to prepare the average full-course meal. From our experience, the upper logs burn with greater vigor than do the andiron logs. They will need to be replenished sooner and more frequently, but this is an easy task requiring only the careful placement of a fresh log or two on the andiron logs.

The andiron logs will not need to be replaced as often, but, when they do, substantial rebuilding and manipulating of the fire's hot logs may be necessary in order to maintain the cooking fire's basic shape. Using green or unseasoned wood for the andiron legs can delay and even eliminate this last step, especially when preparing foods that cook quickly.

For roasting a large piece of meat such as a suckling pig, or for cooking numerous smaller items simultaneously, like ducks, chickens, or Cornish hens, it will be necessary to build a wider or double version of the basic cooking fire. If your fireplace is big enough to accommodate cooking on this scale, a double cooking fire should be adequate for the most ambitious of meals. To build a fire of this design, use three andiron supports, instead of two, and proceed in the same way outlined earlier, with top logs, kindling, etc.

As a general rule, the length of the fire should equal the length of the spitted food in order for the food to roast evenly. And, while this double contiguous fire can be extended further with the addition of more andiron logs, we have rarely found it necessary, nor have we found many fireplaces large enough to contain a fire of this size.

Another important guideline to remember when building a cooking fire is that its size should be governed by the standard length (about eighteen inches) of most pieces of split and cut firewood, and not necessarily by the size of one's fireplace. For example, in a large early American cooking hearth the basic cooking fire, stacked as outlined earlier, measures eighteen inches square. It will appear dwarfed by the enormous proportions of most early fireplaces, but this is fine. The best cooking fires do not fill up the entire hearth area, but leave plenty of free space, so cooking over coals raked apart from the central fire can proceed with ease. If you are fortunate enough to have such an exceptionally spacious hearth, you also might build two of these fires and use one for roasting and the other for your other cooking activities. This was a common practice of the early American housewife and is analogous today to our turning on our oven and cooktop simultaneously.

In the generally smaller modern fireplaces where hearth area is at a premium, the length of the logs used to stack the fire is even more critical. Don't fill up the entire hearth space in your contemporary fireplace with your fire, unless it is absolutely necessary, as doing so will severely limit your cooking possibilities. Should your fireplace be very small, it may be necessary to have your logs cut shorter than the eighteen-inch standard so that the fire does not extend into the room when it has been stacked according to the authors' instructions.

Here is a description of the lengths to which our ancestors went to build fires for preparing their meals and heating their homes. A North American writer is describing his home in New England at the end of the eighteenth century.

> ... the fuel was supplied by our own woods—sweet-scented hickory, snapping chestnut, odoriferous oak, and reeking, fizzling ash—the hot juice of the latter being a sovereign antidote for the ear ache. These were laid in huge piles, all alive with sap, on the tall, gaunt andirons.... The building of the fire was a real architectural achievement, favoured by the wide yawning fireplace, and was always begun by daybreak. There was first a back-log, from fifteen to four and twenty inches in diameter and five feet long, imbedded in the ashes; then came a top-log, then a fore-stick, then a middle-stick, and then a heap of kindlings, reaching from the bowels down to the bottom. A-top of all was a pyramid of smaller fragments, artfully adjusted, with spaces for the blaze.... Friction matches had not then been sent from the regions of brimstone, to enable every boy or begger to carry a conflagration in his pocket. If there were no coals left from last night's fire and none to be borrowed from the neighbors, resort was had to flint, steel, and tinder-box. Often when the fire was dull, and the steel soft and the tinder damp, the striking of fire was a task requiring both energy and patience.*

Another early American fire-building tradition is mentioned in this account—the back-log. The back-log was the name given to the huge green logs that were placed along the rear walls of the kitchen hearth. Some of these logs could better be described as whole small trees, and were reportedly of such immense proportions that they had to be hauled into the kitchen by a team of horses. The back-log served two purposes. It protected the back wall of the fireplace from the deterioration that was caused by the intense heat of the

---

* *Molly Harrison*, The Kitchen in History *(New York: Charles Scribner's Sons, 1972), p. 99.*

constant cooking fires. And, banked with ashes, it safely held smoldering coals overnight, in readiness for lighting the morning fire. In the South, the traditional Yule Log was originally a back-log. The custom arose for the large plantation owners to grant a holiday from chores to their slaves as long as the back-log continued to burn during the Christmas season. Naturally the greener and the bigger a log that could be found, the better. Some of these first Yule logs were said to have lasted for a good week or more.

Regulating the Heat of the Cooking Fire

Today, because we are accustomed to simply turning a dial or pushing a button to achieve a desired oven temperature, it may seem intimidating at first to try to use the comparatively inexact science of cooking with a fire. But we are confident that you can learn to control the fire and to judge its heat with only a little practice and the application of some common sense. Here are some general remarks on this topic to help you avoid burning or undercooking your fireplace dinners. (More detailed information on regulating the cooking heat for specific implements, the tin kitchen, Dutch oven, etc. is given in the practical sections of the technique chapters.)

Regulating the heat of a cooking fire is a two-step process that involves building and maintaining a constant and hot enough fire, then exposing the food to the right amount of heat so that it cooks at a desirable rate.

Maintaining a constant and hot enough fire is the cook's first job and her greatest single control. A fire laid on the hearth in the method outlined earlier in this chapter will generate enough coals approximately one hour after it is ignited for Dutch oven baking, spider frying, or gridiron broiling. Reflector oven roasting, and baking, toasting, and boiling, techniques that rely on the direct and reflected heat of the central fire, can be started somewhat earlier. The cook, then, has only to remember to replenish the fire with additional wood as needed until the cooking is completed.

Once a constant and hot enough fire is reached and maintained and a supply of glowing coals has accumulated, the next step is to judge the amount of coals needed and the best distance from the fire for cooking your food.

For fireplace cooking, and for cooking in general, we have observed that a chef needs only three basic temperatures—low, medium, and high—to prepare practically all foods and recipes successfully. In most cases, variations in temperature of anywhere from 50 to 100 degrees seem to have very little effect on the quality of the finished product, as our experiences with the unreliable thermostat of our supposedly exact electric and gas ovens have proven. And while oven and cooking thermometers can determine the intensity of the fireplace environment and the internal temperature of the cooking food, we have never found such precise measurements necessary. And neither did the original fireplace cooks, who, of course, didn't have such gadgets available to them.

In reality, cooks today are still relying on these same broad heat classifications. On most modern cooktops, the controls are usually marked with only Low, Medium, and High, and we all proceed without hesitation and with little or no difficulty, with only these general guides to follow. Added to this is the irony that, in this era of high technology, professional and gourmet household cooks prefer gas ranges over their electric counterparts, even though they acknowledge that more precise adjustments in temperature are possible with electrical appliances, especially in the lower temperatures, than with gas appliances. Most cooks account for their bias by saying that the flame produced by the gas helps them judge the fire's heat with greater accuracy. Which brings us to the most reliable ways of gauging the heat on your dial-less cooking hearth.

The best way to determine the fire's intensity is for the cook to use her own senses of sight and feeling. As primitive as this may sound, we have found that most cooks have opened their modern ovens enough times—to baste roasting chickens, turn broiling meat, or test a baking cake—to recognize the commonly used oven temperatures by feel. This is invaluable experience in open-hearth cooking, where the cook's skin is constantly exposed to the fire and can serve as a natural thermometer.

Skin sensitivity—combined with the cook's frequent observation of whether the meat or pie crust is browning too quickly or the soup is boiling rather than simmering—should provide sufficient information to allow the cook to select the best distance from the fire for the food or to alter the amount of coals needed to achieve the proper cooking temperature.

Adjustments for raising or lowering the cooking heat when roasting, toasting, and reflector oven baking (techniques that rely on the direct and reflected heat of the fire) can obviously be made by moving the food either closer to or farther away from the fire. When these techniques are being accomplished with implements that rest on the hearth floor, a push towards or away from the central fire will suffice. On the crane, S hooks or trammels enable the fireplace cook to make temperature corrections by raising or lowering the pots of cooking food.

When cooking with coals, adjusting the heat is simply a matter of the quantity of coals used. The fewer the coals under the pots and on their lids, the slower the cooking action; more coals will make for quicker cooking.

While these methods of temperature measurement may seem imprecise, they do work surprisingly well. As Eliza Leslie, the nineteenth-century fireplace cook and author, demonstrated by the inclusion of a soufflé recipe—to be prepared in a Dutch oven, no less—in her famous and highly regarded cookbook. A soufflé is surely one of the more delicate and temperature-sensitive dishes, and a challenge to prepare even with the most sophisticated and predictable sources of cooking heat.

A last observation on coping with the heat of a cooking fire: it takes slightly longer for foods to cook in the fireplace than in a modern appliance. While this may lead to undercooking, fortunately, from our observation, the fireplace cook who does not have exact temperature controls as a guide is naturally more inclined to proceed cautiously. After all, one can always speed up the cooking process by raising the heat, but once the top of the cake is burned, there's no retrieving it!

Safety Precautions at the Hearth

A discussion of the cooking fire would be incomplete without a few words on how to work with it safely.

Although early American women cooked with long-handled pots and utensils, being burned and even burning one's house down were frequent misfortunes, especially in the Colonial period when fireplaces and chimneys were rudely constructed. As a safety measure, these women kept their long, heavy woolen cloaks close at hand to smother any flames in the event they were faced with such an emergency. They were also extremely careful when handling live coals and hot fats. The floor near their cooking hearths was swept constantly, and the hearth itself scrubbed often to keep it free from grease. The twentieth-century cook should emulate these safety measures. Here are some additional precautions for fireplace cooks today.

Make sure your chimney has been checked and cleaned recently for creosote build-up, a common cause of chimney fires and a result of burning green wood and softwoods.

Don't use woods that spark or pop for cooking purposes. In this category, as we have suggested earlier, are the softwoods: cedar, juniper, hemlock, spruce, etc., discussed earlier in this chapter.

Don't use charcoal or synthetic or newspaper logs to cook food. While charcoal can be used safely outdoors, indoors, where toxic fumes can collect, its use can be dangerous. Synthetic or newspaper logs won't produce high enough cooking temperatures or an adequate supply of coals, and may have harmful chemical additives. Avoid lighter fluid or commercial fire starters, too. They can impart a funny taste to your food.

Don't allow roasting or broiling food to drip directly on the hearth. Always use a dripping pan, or improvise one from several thicknesses of aluminum foil, to catch these juices and fats. An accumulation of grease on the hearth will not only create a dreadful mess, but can cause a serious fire, as well.

Don't wear loose clothing that can dangle over or near the flames and catch fire when you are cooking. Sturdy, comfortable shoes are also in order to protect toes from hot embers.

Store ashes in a non-combustible container. (By the way, cold ashes are a beneficial fertilizer for your flower and vegetable gardens.)

Keep a fire extinguisher handy, and know how to use it!

⚜ 3 ⚜

Baking

f the many fireplace cooking
techniques discussed in this book, baking on an open hearth is perhaps the
most foreign to our modern imaginations. Unless one is an ardent camper,
baking a pie or cake with a wood fire has an almost magical quality about it. It
never fails to amaze our dinner guests that everything turns out done to
perfection—the breads rise, the cakes are tender and light, and the pie crusts
evenly browned. And these accomplishments are all achieved without the use
of a thermostatically controlled oven, and in spite of our seemingly casual
attitude about baking times. In order to help you understand how to duplicate
these results yourself, here is a description of what early Americans baked in
their fireplaces and how they did it.

In Early America

Baking, or the use of enclosed heat to cook food, on the first American hearths
was a very uncomplicated process, and the resulting cakes and breads reflected this. They were a far cry from what we are accustomed to eating today.
Corn bread, johnny- or journeycakes, ash cakes, hoecakes, rye n' Injun, and
scratch backs were some of the unfamiliar but amusing-sounding baked foods
consumed in the Colonies. Many of the names aptly describe the distinctive
characteristics of these baked goods, and their method of preparation, as well.

Johnnycakes were "good keepers," staying fresh for a number of days. For
this reason they became a saddlebag staple and were also called journeycakes
by some. Ash cakes were baked, as their name implies, in a wrapping of leaves
amidst the hot fireplace coals. Hoecakes were so-called because they were
baked on the end of a broad iron hoe or shovel, often over an open fire in the

field on a hungry farmer's lunch break. And the rough crust of scratch backs were notorious for scratching the roof of the diner's mouth.

Uniquely American, these breads and cakes were nothing like the delicate, light-textured, perfectly browned, and mild-tasting items we find on our supermarket shelves and in our bakeries today. Frequently just a mixture of cornmeal, grease, water, and salt shaped into small cakes with one's hands, these baked goods were dense from a lack of leavening, strongly flavored from the commonly used molasses sweetener, and often charred by the fire.

How were these early breads and cakes received by the palate of the population? In the 1700's, visiting Englishmen wrote to their relatives that they found them extremely harsh and unpleasant and thought such fare was fit only for slaves. In another period account, a more gracious or perhaps better-fed guest, recorded that he had enjoyed the simple hoecake. But regardless of how they tasted, that these cakes were even edible was a tribute to the Colonial housewife's imagination and ingenuity, and to the cuisine of the American Indian, from which many of her recipes partly derived.

To appreciate fully these breads and cakes, one has to take into account that our first cooks were severely limited by a scarcity of ingredients. Wheat flour, sugar, butter, milk, eggs, and spices—the elementary materials of baking today—were in short supply then, and were often too expensive for daily use when available.

Compounding the problem of the bare larder was the shortage of brick bake ovens, the most sophisticated baking implement of the period. While some villages shared a communal bake oven, more isolated settlers did not enjoy the benefit of such a luxury until the brick-making trade became more firmly established in this country. Also lacking in household kitchens were scales, standardized leavening agents, and measuring spoons and cups.

Pearlash, the first leavening agent (known now as baking powder), even though discovered in the mid-eighteenth century by an American, was regarded with great suspicion at first. Many cooks felt its inclusion in a recipe was harmful to one's health and ruined the flavor of baked goods. Pearlash was originally derived from leaching firewood ashes, so these concerns about its purity and healthfulness may have been well founded.

After the Revolutionary War, when the men were back tending the farms and trade with other nations resumed, the country's economy in general improved, too, and with it, the quality and diversity of baked foods. Fireplace baking from this point on reached culinary heights remarkable even by today's Julia Child standards. It was not uncommon for cookbooks of this era to include recipes for French bread, lady fingers, sponge cake, and puff pastry, or for a variety of such delicacies to grace the tables of wealthy landowners. Sophisticated baking was especially found in the South, which was known for its lavish hospitality and where slaves did the time-consuming and hot work required to prepare beaten biscuits and other specialities at the hearth and in the bake oven.

Among the first baking techniques American women used in their fireplaces was one copied from the native Indian squaws. This technique involved simply sweeping a spot clean on the hearth and placing the unbaked bread or cake, wrapped in corn husks or cabbage leaves, directly on the heated hearth stones or in the fire's coals to cook. A primitive method of baking by any civilization's standards, the resulting baked goods were frequently charred by the fire and coated with ashes.

A refinement of this procedure was to place an inverted iron or crockery pot (sometimes the bottom of the Dutch oven) over the dough. Hot coals were then placed around and heaped on top of this inverted pot to form a crude oven. A makeshift arrangement, this method of baking worked adequately and can successfully be copied in your fireplace today. It can be observed in practice at the re-creation of the 1627 Pilgrim settlement, Plimoth Plantation, in Plymouth, Massachusetts.

Another method of baking that our first housewives employed was to bake their dough on a wooden board. The predecessor of our cookie sheet, this board (almost any piece of sturdy, clean, flat wood qualified) was propped up before the fire in order to cook a layer of dough or thick batter. Bannocks, a flat oatmeal cake of Scottish origin, were traditionally prepared in this manner. Hence the baking board came to be called a Bannock board by many. Other foods could be baked on these boards, as well. Eliza Leslie recommends this method of preparation in the following recipe for johnnycake from her *Directions for Cookery, In Its Various Branches:*

Johnny Cake

Sift a quart of Indian meal into a pan; make a hole in the middle, pour in a pint of warm water. Mix the meal and water gradually into a batter, adding a small teaspoon of salt. Beat it very hard, and for a long time, till it becomes quite light. Then spread it thick and even on a stout piece of smooth board. Place it upright on the hearth before a clear fire, with a flat iron or something of the sort to support the board behind, and bake it well. Cut it into squares, and split and butter them hot.

While the authors have not personally tested Miss Leslie's johnnycake recipe, we have tried to duplicate this baking technique. We must confess that we found it impossible to achieve satisfactory results by baking on a board, and can't recommend it with confidence to the modern cook. Our repeated efforts were plagued with uneven baking, and cookies that slowly slid down the board, no matter how slight its incline, onto the hearth before the baking was completed. Letting the cakes "set" or dry out first, by placing the board in a horizontal position before the fire, as was suggested in a recent twentieth-century article on fireplace cooking, didn't solve this problem for us, either.

Among the most reliable devices developed for fireplace baking, devices which were widely used by everyday housewives of moderate means to accomplish this task, were the Dutch oven, reflector oven, and baking griddle. A description of these implements and their use is given in the practical section of this chapter, which follows. These utensils give reliable results, are simple to use, and, with the exception of the griddle, are relatively inexpensive, since reproductions of their antique models are currently being produced.

But before we turn to their use, and to baking today in your fireplace, we would like to describe the most advanced baking oven developed during the fireplace cooking era—the beehive oven.

Beehive ovens, as their name suggests, were large dome- or beehive-shaped brick compartments in which cakes, breads, and other foods whose flavors were enhanced by a steady, moderate heat, were baked. In the earliest fireplaces, as we have seen, beehive ovens were built behind the cooking hearth with their doors opening into the back wall of the fireplace at approximately waist level. In order to preheat, test, insert, or remove food from these ovens, the cook actually had to step onto, or at best lean over, the hearth, bringing her long, full skirts dangerously close to the ever-present central cooking fire.

In later fireplaces, this design was modified, and bake ovens were built to one side of the fireplace, so that their doors were now located on the wall next to the hearth, and they opened directly into the room. Here the cook didn't have to enter the hearth fire area when using the bake oven, a safer and more convenient arrangement.

These indoor bake ovens shared the central fireplace chimney flue as a means of draft. Their doors were at first just slabs of wood, pushed into place, which tightly fitted the mouths of the ovens. These were latter replaced by non-flammable and more durable iron doors properly hinged to the oven opening. In hotter climates bake ovens were frequently separate structures built entirely outside the main house, with their own sheds to protect both them and the cooks on baking day from the elements.

Baking breads and cakes and other foods in the beehive oven produced, with practice and experience, delicious and predictable results, but it was an arduous and time-consuming task. Depending on the size of one's family, baking in this oven was undertaken only once or at the very most twice a week.

To bake in this oven, one had to first preheat or "fire" it. Firing the oven was literally what preheating entailed. A fire of special oven wood was built directly on the bake oven's brick floor. Oven wood was merely dry, hardwood cut into small pieces of equal length. The wood was often reserved expressly for bake oven fires. This fire was kept burning inside the oven until the oven had reached the desired baking temperature—a process which sometimes took up the greater part of the day. During the preheating period the fire was frequently replenished, stoked, and its coals re-distributed to produce even heating of the oven's bricks. While the oven was heating the cooks used the time to prepare the large quantities of pies, cakes, breads, and other foods to be baked in it later.

Oven temperature was determined by the "bare arm" method, or by "trying" the oven with a bit of flour. The bare arm technique is described in an early cookbook as follows:

> For pies, cakes, and white bread, the heat of the oven should be such that you can hold your hand and arm (in it) while you count to 40; for brown bread, meats, beans, Indian puddings, and pumpkin pies, it should be hotter, so that you can only hold it in while you count to 20.*

To try the oven with flour, the cook sprinkled a handful on its floor and noted the rate at which it browned. If the flour browned too quickly or burned, the oven was too hot, and if it browned too slowly, it was too cold.

Obviously, experience counted!

When the oven was deemed hot enough, the remains of the fire were removed with a long-handled ash shovel, and its floor was swept clean. Next, fresh leaves were spread on the oven's floor and a layer of cornmeal was dusted over them. This prevented the unbaked bread dough, pies, and cakes from sticking to the oven's floor or scorching, since most cooks did not own enough baking pans to accommodate all the baked goods the oven held at one firing.

To cool slightly the hot roof of the oven, and to remove any lingering stray ashes that might drift down and stick to the surface of the baking foods, the upper part of the oven was quickly brushed with a wet broom. The steam created by its moisture also produced a lovely glazed crust on the baked goods.

Foods requiring the hottest temperatures were baked first. These generally included breads, cakes, and pies. When these were completed and removed, successive loads which needed more moderate heat were put in the oven and allowed to cook slowly, occasionally overnight. Among the foods in this latter category were crocks of beans, casseroles, and pumpkin and Indian puddings. And even when the oven had become too cool for "cooking" food, its remaining warmth was sometimes utilized by the thrifty homemaker to dry her herbs.

While these brick ovens produced excellent results, we should add that they generally were to be found only in the more comfortable households—and, of course, in professional bakeries. But it was known practice for homemakers of more modest means to pay their local baker to bake their foods in his beehive oven for them.

Techniques For Today

Thus far we have described opposite ends of the spectrum concerning fireplace baking techniques. But, since the majority of us do not live in restorations with beehive bake ovens, and are not interested in reverting to a charred

* *Molly Harrison*, The Kitchen In History *(New York: Charles Scribner's Sons, 1972)*

caveman cuisine, exemplified earlier by the ash cake and baking board, we have focused the practical section of this chapter on baking in your fireplace today using the methods of early American housewives.

The average woman of yesterday accomplished her daily baking (as did her more affluent neighbors who owned bake ovens, when they wished to prepare only a few items) with the Dutch oven, reflector oven, and hanging griddle. We will first describe the technique of baking in the Dutch oven, as it is a most versatile piece of equipment, almost foolproof to use, and does not require a fireplace crane to support it. Most important, of the three baking implements mentioned, the Dutch oven disperses heat most evenly on all surfaces of foods baked in it.

Before we delve into the specific use of the Dutch oven, here are some general observations on baking in your fireplace which are true for all three implements.

Don't worry too much about exact oven temperatures. We have intentionally omitted them from this book, and we feel they are particularly irrelevant for baking. Instead, we have indicated low, medium, and high heats for the recipes. If you are very hesitant about this informal approach, a portable oven thermometer could be placed inside the Dutch oven or on the shelf of the reflector oven until you become more experienced and comfortable with approximating correct fireplace baking temperatures. We have never used an oven thermometer for fireplace baking, however, and don't think you will find one necessary.

The placement of the Dutch oven, reflector oven, and hanging griddle in relation to the fire, and the amount of coals needed for baking as described in this chapter, have been determined for a moderate oven, about 325–350 degrees. If you are substituting one of your own recipes when trying out any of these techniques, you may have to adjust the heat accordingly, although we have found that most foods can be successfully baked using this one average temperature range.

Judgment and caution are especially important in fireplace baking. We recommend that you check your baking food frequently to be sure that it is progressing to your satisfaction. The greatest danger in baking, and one whose damages cannot be remedied, is for cooking to proceed too rapidly with too much heat, causing the outside of food to be done before the inside is thoroughly cooked.

In short, while most anything can be baked in the fireplace using Dutch oven, reflector oven, and hanging griddle, large cakes and the more delicate ones, such as angel food or chiffon, should probably be avoided, unless you are very experienced or courageous. Even Eliza Leslie cautioned her expert fireplace cooking audience:

It is safest when practicable, to send all large cakes to a professional baker. . . .
It may be recommended to novices in the art of baking, to do everything in little

tins or in very shallow pans; there being then less risk than with a large thick cake.

The Dutch Oven

Dutch ovens, beehive ovens notwithstanding, were the best all-around baking devices of the fireplace cooking era. Unlike the ones sold today for use with modern cooktops and ovens, the original Dutch oven had three short legs, a lid with a raised edge, and usually a bail, another name for a handle. Although this version has long since disappeared from our kitchens, you may recall it from your scout or camping days, for it is still commonly used in campfire cooking.

Following is the basic technique for baking in the Dutch oven, which in the authors' estimation is still the foremost implement available for fireplace baking today.

One hour before you plan to begin baking in your Dutch oven, lay and ignite your fire as described in Chapter 2, The Cooking Fire. This will allow adequate time for the fire to produce the coals necessary to begin baking. Roughly two small shovelfuls, or enough coals to form a single layer under the oven and on its lid, are needed to achieve a temperature suitable for baking in the Dutch oven. Some more coals will be needed later to sustain its heat until the contents are done. When you have judged the fire to have produced these coals, it's time to preheat your oven.

To preheat the Dutch oven, pick a convenient spot on the hearth for the baking to take place, and shovel a small amount of hot coals here. A good location for baking is one that is easily accessible to the cook, but where she won't trip over the oven, and one that is not too close to the central fire. Place the oven, lid on, over these coals and shovel more coals onto its lid. Ten minutes later your oven will be sufficiently preheated and ready for baking.

The recipe mixture should then be poured into the appropriately sized and shaped pan and placed on a wire rack inside the Dutch oven. Sometimes, if the baking pan fits snugly inside the oven, to avoid spills or burned fingers, it may be easier to reverse this step, by placing the empty pan or pie shell and rack inside the oven first, and then pouring or placing your batter into its container. This suggestion is especially helpful for custard and pumpkin pie fillings, and the more liquid cake batters.

The wire rack mentioned is essential for successful Dutch oven baking. It permits air circulation beneath the food being baked, prevents scorching of the bottoms of your pies, cakes, and breads, and avoids damage to your Pyrex and pottery pans, which may break on direct contact with the intense heat of the oven's iron bottom. It is also important to note here that Dutch ovens are not sold with this vital accessory.

Historically, in place of this wire rack, cooks tempered the heat of the Dutch oven's iron floor by covering its bottom with a layer of ashes or sand. And while we are sure that this worked well for them, our preference is a circular cake rack, the kind used for cooling cakes and cookies. Only the largest Dutch ovens will accommodate these racks, but the authors have used wire Christmas wreath forms with great success in smaller ovens. Campers frequently use bottle caps or crumpled foil on the bottoms of their Dutch ovens to create the same effect.

After the baking mixture is safely in the oven on its rack, replace the lid and replenish the coals, top and bottom, placing slightly more coals on the lid or underneath to distribute the oven's heat appropriately for the food to be baked. The chart at the end of this section details the proportionate amount of coals for baking most recipes.

Be very careful not to burn yourself when maneuvering the hot, heavy lid of the Dutch oven. Use a very thick potholder, or, even better, an asbestos barbecue mitt, to protect your hands. A bale hook with a wooden handle is also handy for this task. Such hooks can often be bought inexpensively at flea markets from dealers who specialize in antique or just old tools and farm implements.

Now, leave the oven alone, letting it bake for about thirty minutes, or until the coals turn white and are no longer heating it. Then add more fresh coals from the fire, and, holding the entire Dutch oven by its handle, rotate it 180 degrees. This rotation prevents the food from becoming overcooked on the side facing the central fire. Turning the Dutch oven may be an optional step, depending on the proximity of the fire to the implement. In a large fireplace, the heat of the central cooking fire may not affect the oven's temperature, especially if the oven is "baking" on the far edge of the hearth.

When indicated in your recipe, test the food for doneness in the standard way, such as with a cake tester or by tapping the tops of the bread loaves. When removing or replacing the lid of the Dutch oven, be very careful not to drop ashes or coals on your food.

After your baking is completed, "turn off" the oven by removing its lid. This is a very important step. It not only helps to stop the baking action, but prevents moisture from accumulating on the underside of the lid and dripping on to your food, giving it a peculiar flavor. Next, move the bottom of the oven (food inside) away from the coals and fire. When the food is cool, lift out your Dutch-oven-baked treat and enjoy your creation!

After you have mastered the basic routine just outlined for baking in your Dutch oven, you many want to try some of the following interesting variations on its use.

If you own two Dutch ovens, one preferably smaller than the other, you can bake in both of them simultaneously by stacking the smaller one on top of the larger. Baking in this double oven not only requires fewer coals (the coals on the lower lid serve to heat the bottom of the upper oven) and uses less hearth space, but allows you to bake desserts and bread at the same time. For ease in checking the progress of the baking, be sure to place the food with the longest cooking time in the bottom oven.

One can also bake successfully in a Dutch oven without using a cake pan or rack. The corn bread recipe included in the recipe section of this book turns out well prepared this way. Without a pan, the finished product has a rather free-form shape, but this doesn't diminish its flavor, quality, or ease in baking.

To bake directly on the bottom of your Dutch oven, you'll need to line it first either with leaves or heavy paper. For lack of paper, the early American housewife lined her oven with fresh maple leaves, when they were available. They left a pretty star-shaped pattern on the bottom of her baked goods, and the stems were natural handles for removing the lining when the baking was completed. In the dead of winter when the maple trees were bare, the more flexible leaves of a head of cabbage would do. In the fall, the housewife often sent her children a-leafing to collect maple leaves for use over the winter months. These were threaded on long strings and hung from the kitchen rafters to preserve them until they were needed.

Approximate Oven Temperatures and Distribution of Coals for Dutch Oven Baking

Biscuits. High heat. Evenly distribute an equal amount of coals on lid of oven and underneath it throughout baking.

Breads. Moderate to high heat. For first half of baking, evenly distribute an equal amount of coals on lid of oven and underneath it. For second half of baking, place slightly more coals on lid of oven to brown top crust.

Cakes. Moderate heat. Evenly distribute an equal amount of coals on lid of oven and underneath it throughout baking.

Cookies. High heat. Evenly distribute an equal amount of coals on lid of oven and underneath it throughout baking.

Custards. Moderate heat. Place slightly more coals on lid of oven than underneath it throughout baking.

Fruits. Moderate heat. Evenly distribute an equal amount of coals on lid of oven and underneath it throughout baking.

Muffins. Moderate heat. Evenly distribute an equal amount of coals on lid of oven and underneath it throughout baking.

Pies. Moderate to high heat. For first half of baking, place slightly more coals underneath oven than on top to set bottom crust. For second half of baking, reverse this, placing slightly more coals on lid of oven to brown top crust.

The modern housewife may want to stash some maple leaves in her freezer instead of hanging them from her ceiling, as we find this preserves them better. Although not as charming as maple leaves, several layers of brown paper cut from grocery bags to fit the oven's bottom and greased will also serve to line the Dutch oven effectively.

After lining the oven, pour or place your bread or cake mixture directly into it and proceed with the baking as described earlier. After the baking is completed, and the oven cool enough to handle, invert its bottom over a cutting board, allowing the baked foods to gently fall out. Carefully peel off the liner and you're ready to eat.

The Reflector Oven

The reflector bake oven, or tin kitchen, was another baking device American women used in their fireplaces. Introduced to the cooking hearth after the Dutch oven, it was supposedly an improvement over its predecessor. But it never gained the same degree of popularity for baking. This was probably because these new ovens were considered an "extra" by the generally frugal housewives who already owned a very adequate and indestructible iron Dutch oven. And, in practice, not only did the reflector oven not bake quite as evenly as the Dutch oven, but it was not as versatile a cooking device. A cook could stew, fry, boil, bake, and perform most every cooking technique, except roasting, in her Dutch oven, while with a reflector bake oven she was limited to baking.

Tin kitchens or reflector ovens modified for roasting, on the other hand, were quickly accepted in the open-hearth kitchen, and were hailed by food authorities as the ultimate roasting device for fireplace cooking. The only difference between reflector ovens for roasting and those for baking was that the former were fitted with spits for suspending meat rather than with a shelf for holding breads, pies, cakes and other baked goods.

Reflector oven baking.

Unlike the Dutch oven, which is still being produced for campers and is available from many outlets including the Boy Scouts of America, the reflector bake oven is a scarce commodity. Antique versions are rare and expensive, and, while reproductions for camping use are reasonably priced, we know of only one source in the United States that currently produces and sells them, namely Sims Stoves (see Chapter 10, Sources For Equipping A Fireplace Kitchen).

But, if you are at all handy, it is not too difficult to build a reflector oven. Plans for constructing one have appeared in the magazine, *Early American Life*. To obtain these instructions, see Chapter 10. For a description of how to improvise a reflector bake oven from aluminum foil and other common household materials see *Backcountry Cooking*, by J. Wayne Fears published by the East Woods Press.

The reflector bake oven, difficult as it may be to obtain, does offer some special advantages over the Dutch oven for the modern fireplace cook. For these reasons we have included a discussion of its use in this section. The reflector oven's pluses are five. It does not need to be preheated before baking can begin, and it does not rely on coals to supply the baking heat. These factors speed the time when cooking can begin. The reflector oven takes up less hearth space than the Dutch oven, an important consideration with today's generally smaller fireplaces. It is lighter in weight than the Dutch oven, hence easier to handle. And it is cleaner to use, since its use involves no shoveling of ashes or coals before or after baking, a decisive factor if your fireplace happens to be in an elegant setting.

The modern-day reflector oven and its nineteenth-century antecedent work on the same principle. They rely on the reflected and direct heat of the fire to bake their foods. Both models are constructed of shiny metal (tin) to promote the greatest reflection of the fire's heat from their walls onto the food. The modern, although not widely available, camping version of the reflector bake oven resembles a large V resting on its side. It has small feet and an interior central shelf for holding the food. The original fireplace reflector ovens were shaped like cylinders sliced in half lengthwise, but they too had small feet and a shelf spanning their midsections.

To bake in these ovens, just put your dough or batter into a pan and place it on the oven's shelf; if you are baking cookies or biscuits, they may be set directly on the shelf, and the shelf may be greased or not as your recipes direct for the preparation of the cookie sheet or baking pan. Then place the oven, open end facing the fire, on the hearth floor about eight to ten inches from the heat to bake. This distance varies depending on the intensity of the fire and the reflecting ability of the oven's walls. A dirty oven, or an old one that has lost its shine, will not bake as efficiently as a bright, new one.

To judge the temperature, or readiness of the fire for reflector oven baking, here is a variation on the bare arm method used by the beehive oven bakers, from the current Boy Scout handbook.

Place your hand over the fire, and count in the following fashion: "one and one, two and two, etc." When you can no longer hold your hand over the heat, gauge the fire's temperature according to the following chart:

Hand removed at a count of:

6 — 8   low (250 degrees)
4 — 5   medium (350 — 400 degrees)
2 — 3   hot (400 — 450 degrees)
1 or less very hot (450 — 500 degrees)

It is very important when using a reflector oven to check the progress of the baking food frequently. This is most easily and safely accomplished by very gently pulling the oven away from the fire, with pot-holder–protected hands, for a quick look at the food. To raise or lower the baking temperature, one has only to move the oven closer to or further away from the heat.

Test your baking food for doneness in the conventional way at the time indicated in your recipe. When your cooking is completed, move the oven a comfortable distance away from the fire and remove the bread, cookies, etc., to a rack to cool.

If you really like this baking technique, and if your fireplace is large enough, next try baking in two reflector ovens at one time. Place the ovens on the hearth so that they face one another with the cooking fire built between them. Lay the fire sideways so that the oven openings are in front of the tunnel opening formed by stacked logs. Place uncooked food on shelves of both ovens and allow to bake. Follow tips outlined above for baking in a single reflector oven.

Two ovens, used as described, are supposed to be super-efficient, multiplying the potential surfaces for the fire's heat to reflect and deflect from, and thereby increasing their baking action.

The Hanging Griddle

If you are lucky enough to already have a crane or an adjustable trammel in your fireplace, or are thinking about installing either of them, then you can also try baking on a griddle. Early American bake griddles were round, flat iron plates with large curved handles and swivel hooks by which the cook suspended them over the fire to bake her food. The swivel hook allowed the cook to turn the griddle baking surface in order to even out its heat and to easily bring all of the baking food within her reach. Some versions of the bake griddle had short feet so that the implement would also rest firmly on the fireplace floor. And still other models were constructed so that they were collapsible. The baking surface in these was hinged so that it folded into the same plane as the handle when not in use.

Griddle baking was an interesting baking method and one that has fallen into disuse in our modern kitchens. One of the few remnants of this technique which still remains today is the practice of baking pancakes in our frying pans.

"Baking" pancakes on the hanging griddle. French toast, bannocks, and English muffins can be baked this way at your hearth.

But griddle baking had obvious limitations, even in early American homes. It would, for example be hard to imagine baking a layer cake or a hearty loaf of bread on a griddle. Its areas of best use were in the preparation of small baked goods: cookies, biscuits, muffins, and cupcakes.

Antique bake griddles were widely used on cooking hearths, and are still plentiful in antique shops today. Reproductions of this implement though, are not being mass produced, to our knowledge, so one would have to commission a blacksmith to make a copy for you, if in your travels you did not uncover an authentic one.

Here's how to bake on the griddle. Hang it from the crane or trammel so that its baking plate sits about 1 1/2 to 2 feet above the logs of a well-established cooking fire. The griddle should not hang in the fire's flames. Preheat the griddle in this position for about ten minutes. When it is hot, place your biscuit dough or other unbaked food on it. Let the food bake undisturbed for the length of time indicated in the recipe, turn, if necessary, and then remove a sample with a metal spatula or tongs to test for doneness. Be careful not to tip the griddle when you are performing this last step or you will have made ash cakes. During baking you may need to adjust the height of the griddle in order to increase or decrease the baking temperature. Different lengths of pothooks or an adjustment in the trammel will accomplish this. The cook may also have to turn the griddle if one area of the baking surface is hotter than another.

Baking "rings" were a common accessory used on baking griddles during the fireplace cooking period. Small rings about 1 1/2 inches in diameter and 1 inch high, they were forms for containing the more liquid batters baked on the griddle. These rings can easily be improvised in a few moments from several thicknesses of heavy aluminum foil folded into one-inch strips with their ends pinched, clipped, or stapled together to form a circle. Empty seven-ounce tuna or salmon cans with their bottoms as well as their tops removed can also serve as baking rings. Rings sold for baking English crumpets can be ordered from the Williams–Sonoma catalogue listed in Chapter 10.

The Waffle and Wafer Iron

Waffle and wafer irons were common accessories in early American fireplaces. They produced delicious baked desserts that were consumed with great relish at the hearth (often as fast as the cook could make them), and were served topped or filled with sweetened fruit or jam and whipped cream, or dipped in honey. Both the waffle and wafer iron cooked batter or dough by pressing it between two preheated, patterned iron plates that were hinged together. These plates were attached to long handles, which enabled the cook to heat the irons at a comfortable distance from the fire and allowed her to extract them safely and easily when they reached the appropriate temperature for baking.

Waffle irons were designed to hold a looser batter than wafer irons. They were usually rectangular or round, although some were heart-shaped, and their baking surfaces were cast in a deep grid design, the traditional waffle pattern. The light, crispy, cake-like waffles baked in them were comparable to those we eat today.

By comparison, wafer iron baking plates were usually round or rectangular and their baking surfaces were decorated with a variety of delicate designs. Commonly pictured were birds, flowers, hearts, a bride's initials, or even religious motifs, since these irons were also used to make wafers for sacramental purposes. Unlike waffle irons, the baking surfaces of the wafer iron were essentially flat, as these patterns were only shallowly incised. A small, stiff ball of sweetened dough (or a finger of dough, depending on the iron's shape) was pressed between its two plates, as a more liquid batter would have run off its shallow surfaces. The resulting wafers resembled thin, crispy, and very pretty cookies.

Like most antiques, authentic waffle and wafer irons are scarce. Especially coveted by collectors are the more ornately decorated ones. So your chances of finding one of these irons at a reasonable price are rather remote. But similar baking irons are still being used and produced by other cultures around the world, and these can be used in your fireplace, although their manufacturers generally include directions for their use only on modern cooktops. A Belgian waffle iron with a non-stick coating on its baking surface and a temperature gauge, and an Italian pizzelle iron for making fluted wafers, were both offered in a recent Williams–Sonoma catalogue, an excellent mail-order source for unusual cooking equipment. The firm's address is given in Chapter 10, Sources for Equipping Your Cooking Fireplace. Similar irons can also probably be found in a well-stocked gourmet or kitchen supplies shop or in the housewares section of larger department stores such as Bloomingdale's.

Using a waffle or wafer iron is surprisingly simple. First you must season its cooking surfaces by rubbing them with a coating of vegetable oil or shortening. Next, the iron is preheated by resting it for a few minutes over a healthy bed of glowing coals or on the top log of the cooking fire. It should take about three to five minutes to preheat the iron, and it should be turned over midway during the heating process so both sides of the iron are equally heated. (A drop of water will sizzle on the cooking surface of the iron when it is ready for baking). Next, remove the iron from the fire, and rest it on a trivet or log near the edge

Preheating waffle iron in coals.

Waffle iron with cooked waffle. Gridiron or green log is good to rest waffle or wafer iron on to remove baked product.

of the hearth. Open it, and add your batter (for a waffle) or ball of dough (for a wafer). Close the iron and let it "cook" undisturbed until steam stops coming out its sides, another two to three minutes. This time will vary depending on the size of the iron and the temperature of its baking surface. Then open the iron, being careful not to burn your fingers, and gently pry the wafer or waffle away from the sides of the iron with the tines of a fork or the tip of a sharp knife, and serve. For wafers, many early American recipes suggest rolling the cookie while it is still warm and pliable, and then filling it when cool, with whipped cream, and adding a bit of jam or a fresh strawberry at either end to serve as a decorative and tasty stopper. Repeat for each waffle and wafer desired, until your mixture is used up.

The amount of dough or batter to use for each waffle and wafer will be determined largely by the size of your iron. You will have to experiment a little to come up with an exact measurement. Usually for a standard-sized and -shaped wafer iron, a ball of dough the size of a walnut is adequate, and for a waffle iron about 1/8-cup of batter will suffice. It is better to estimate slightly less for your first trials, as overflowing batter will make quite a mess on your hearth. Reseason the iron as needed—usually after every three or four waffles or wafers is often enough.

Indian-Style Baking

Last but not least, we feel we can't omit a short mention of the simplest of all baking techniques, baking food right in the fire's hot coals, Indian-style.

As we observed earlier, Indian-style is not a satisfactory technique for baking cakes, pies, breads or baked goods in general. Almost any other basic food, however, can be easily and tastily prepared in this way. The possibilities are really endless, from baked apples to baked chicken. Indian-style baking is also a technique that children can participate in and will enjoy. And it can provide the inspiration for an Indian birthday party lunch, an imaginative and delicious alternative to fast food.

To prepare foods for baking in the coals, replace the green corn husks, cabbage leaves, and parchment, which the Indians and our first settlers used for wrapping their foods, with aluminum foil.

Select basic foods to cook in this manner. Acorn squash, ears of corn, yams, or chicken legs would be good choices. Add butter and seasonings as your tastes dictate. Then wrap small amounts or individual portions of the food carefully in several layers of foil, sealing the edges well. Next, sit the packages on a layer of hot coals to cook, placing a few more coals on the tops of these packages, as well, so that tops and bottoms bake evenly.

When the food is finished cooking, or when you are checking its progress by slitting the top of the package or carefully unwrapping it, take care not to pierce the bottom layer of foil as you will lose all the delicious juices inside. A spatula or wooden tongs are good tools for this last step.

Now sit cross-legged, Indian-style, around the fire and feast!

4

Roasting, Toasting, Broiling, and Browning Off

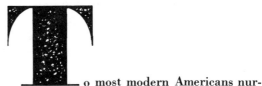

o most modern Americans nurtured on food cooked with gas, electricity, and microwaves, one of the unexpected and unparalleled delights of fireplace cooking is that food broiled, toasted, but most especially roasted before a wood fire develops a pleasing and unique flavor. It's a flavor that has never been equalled by any other more advanced cooking method, fuel, or device—the charcoal barbecue included.

Early American housewives took this benefit rather lightly, or perhaps they were just exhausted from the backbreaking labor required of their ground-level hearths—the standard design of most cooking fireplaces that were built in this country. Whatever the most compelling reason, American women (the ones who could afford to) readily abandoned their kitchen fireplaces for the revolutionary wood-burning cookstoves introduced in the early 1800's. It is amusing to interject here that a few staunch supporters of the flavor of fireplace-cooked food were convinced that these new-fangled devices would never gain broad acceptance. Food prepared on them simply didn't taste as good as when it was prepared in the old-fashioned manner, at the hearth.

Although there was a lot of truth to such claims, these voices were very much in the minority, and were most likely not those of the household cooks. As history has recorded, progress prevailed, and the American fascination for kitchen gadgetry produced dramatically new methods of mechanized meal preparation. An overwhelming array of devices, designed to improve and simplify our lives, have all but engulfed our kitchens, and have pressed wood as a cooking fuel into virtual extinction. While we are not suggesting that you toss your modern conveniences into the garbage and resurrect a fireplace for everyday cooking, we do feel there is something to be enjoyed and gained by following some of the cooking techniques of the past that we have been too quick to discard as outmoded. This is especially true for roasting.

In many European countries, by comparison, and in more exotic parts of the world as well, roasting with a wood fire has remained through the years a highly regarded cooking technique and one which is still practiced in many private homes and in some of the finest restaurants. And, only lately, a growing interest and sophistication about food among Americans has prompted in our more cosmopolitan cities the appearance of restaurants where true roasting has been revived, and where one can experience the delectable flavor of food cooked before a wood fire.

Roasting In Early America

Historically, fireplace cooks defined roasting quite differently from the way we define it today. In fact, early cooking authorities would have considered our modern method of roasting more like baking. Today, the meat is placed in the oven, resting on a rack in a shallow pan, with a small amount of water covering the bottom. This is described as a procedure for preparing a plain baked dish, one which is suitable for the family table.

Fireplace era roasting was described in 1770 by Martha Bradley, author of *The British Housewife*, a book known to have been circulated in the Colonies, as "dressing food before a naked fire." Positioning food directly over flames or coals to be roasted was not desirable, as it allowed dripping fat and juices from the meat to fall on the fire or coals. This produced billowing smoke and spitting flames that engulfed the food, affected its flavor, and irritated the cook's eyes.

Early food writers were also quite specific in their directions regarding the quality and preparations necessary for a good roasting fire. To quote Eliza Leslie: "A roasting fire should be prepared at least one half hour before the roast is put down." (From our own experience, more like forty-five minutes is needed to allow for the less proficient fire-building skills of the modern cook.) "It [the fire]," she continued, "should be large, steady, clear, and bright with plenty of fine hot coals at the bottom." "Your [roasting] fire must also be made in proportion to the piece you are to dress. . . .," wrote Susannah Carter. And fireplace cooks generally agreed that a large blaze filling the entire hearth accomplished nothing except to overheat the cook and the room. The location of the fire on the hearth was also commented upon. The best spot for roasting (remember, these references are to the oversized, often cavernous cooking fireplaces of yesterday) was near the front of the fireplace and off to one side of it. Here, the roast could be easily reached for turning and basting without its presence interfering with the housewife's other cooking activities.

Fireplace era cookbooks also offered early cooks a number of guidelines to follow when preparing their meat for roasting. These directions are summarized below. They apply to roasting beef in particular, but they were also applicable to a leg of lamb, whole turkey, and even a haunch of venison. A few of these suggestions may seem curious and puzzling to the modern reader, but many of the others are still very relevant for fireplace roasting today. Still, they are included here more for their historical interest than for their practical importance.

Washing meat in cold water, wiping it dry, and rubbing it with salt were Eliza Leslie's method of preparing a roast for the spit. Even then, however, the application of salt before cooking commenced was controversial. Other early food writers warned that salting meat too soon in the cooking process drew out its juices and ruined the roast, an opinion held by many cooks today.

Another roasting practice of early cooks was to tie blank paper over the fat of the roast. The purpose of the paper covering was to prevent the fat from melting away, or "wasting too fast," the old cooks said.

Care was also taken to position the roast at the proper distance from the fire. The outside of the meat could become burned before the inside was cooked if it was placed too close to the heat (good, practical advice that holds true today, as well).

Twenty minutes per pound was used by chefs of the later fireplace cooking era to estimate the length of time to roast their meat. Cooking time, naturally, varied with the size of the roast, with the tastes (for rare or well-done meat) of the diners, and curiously enough, with the season of the year. In summer, it was observed, a roast cooked faster than in the winter months. This is a point the authors will accept at face value, as we don't intend to verify this information by preparing a fireplace meal on a typical, eighty-five degree, humid, New Jersey August day.

Another interesting observation of early cooks was that steam from the roast "drew" towards the fire when the roast was done. Such information was probably more useful for the homemaker before cooking timers, scales, and oven thermometers were at her disposal.

And finally, another widespread practice that has fallen out of use today was for cooks to dredge a roast lightly with flour and a little melted butter when its cooking neared completion. This produced a delicate froth on the surface of the meat which supposedly enhanced its appearance.

To suspend, support, and rotate the haunches of venison, hindquarters of bear, whole 'coons, woodchucks, wild turkeys, and the meat of the other wild and domesticated animals that were roasted in American fireplaces, many ingenious and elaborate devices were invented and used by early cooks. Some of these roasting aides even incorporated their own dripping pans, reflecting panels, and turning mechanisms.

The simplest of these roasting implements, and one which can be easily duplicated and used today, was improvised from only a long length of stout cord or a thin strip of rawhide. Using one end of the cord, the cook trussed her fowl or tied her piece of meat into a neat and secure package. She then tied the other end of this cord to a nail or hook in the fireplace mantel or chimney throat so that the food hung directly in front of a hot fire. An occasional prod with her large meat fork caused the cord to wind and then unwind on itself.

The motion exposed all sides of the food to the fire, browning and cooking it evenly with very little attention from the chef.

The cord method, as well as all the other devices used to roast food in the fireplace, with the exception of the tin kitchen, required that a pan be placed under the cooking meat to catch its dripping fat and juices. These pans, called dripping pans, served a dual purpose. They not only prevented fat from accumulating on the hearth and perhaps causing serious fire, but they also collected the drippings, which the cook used to baste her roasting food, and the grease, which was saved to make rush lights and candles.

While roasting with a hanging cord was simple and effective, its major drawback was that one could not cook on a string the abundant and delicate-fleshed fish that this country's settlers enjoyed and often relied upon for survival. To roast fish, the earliest fireplace cooks resorted instead to a technique known as "planking." Copied from the American Indian cooking, planking involved tying the whole fish or its fillets to a slab of hard, preferably fruit or nut wood. This improvised cooking sheet was then propped at an angle before the fire to roast the food. A heavy object such as log, stone, or iron pot was used to support the plank in the desired position.

This procedure works as well today as it did yesterday for all kinds of fish, a food which, in general, cooks rather quickly. But it was inadequate then, as now, for roasting the denser, slower-cooking flesh of domestic livestock and wild game, since after a prolonged period before the fire, the plank began to roast along with the food.

An improvement over these two primitive methods—the cord and the plank—was the spit. A fireplace utensil versatile enough for roasting both meat and fish, it became the standard roasting implement for the fireplace cook.

The first spits, used in the poorest homes and in the most primitive settings, were probably just sturdy green branches with one end sharpened to a point to spear the roasting food. The cook either held this spit in her hand while cooking dinner or anchored it at an angle before the fire with rocks. Roasting in this manner is familiar to scouts and campers, who still use this method of cooking at campsites. But for daily fireplace cooking, it was at best a makeshift arrangement. The branch could support only small pieces of food, and the cook ran the risk of her spit burning and breaking before her cooking was completed.

As blacksmiths became more common, branch spits were replaced with iron ones, the simplest of which closely resembled the sharpened branch just described. These spits were forged, spear-like pieces of iron two to three feet in length, with two short feet that supported the spit in an unbalanced seesaw position before the fire. The food was impaled on the raised end of the spit. Although generally very crudely formed, sometimes the handle ends of these spits were embellished by a creative blacksmith with fanciful designs or formed into a heart or other decorative shape. But while the iron version of the branch spit had the advantage of not catching fire as did its antecedent, it still could hold only smaller pieces of food before the fire, and it sometimes became extremely hot and hard to handle.

A major improvement on the iron spear spit was the horizontal iron spit. The horizontal spit could support larger cuts of meat, as well as fish, and also permitted the cook to turn them with ease before the fire. The horizontal iron spit was supported before the fire on hooks which protruded from vertical sections of special cooking andirons. A series of hook-rests were attached at different levels on the verticals of the andirons to allow the cook to raise or lower the spit, adjusting its distance from the fire and the cooking temperature of the food. Most fireplace kitchens were equipped with several iron spits in varying lengths and thicknesses from which the cook selected one appropriate for the size of her roast.

Another, more unusual, way of suspending the horizontal roasting spit in the fireplace can be observed at Hopewell Village in Elverson, Pennsylvania. Hopewell Village was a major iron-forging community in the 1700's, and has been restored to its former appearance and designated as a National Historic Site. In this recreated eighteenth-century setting, food is roasted over glowing coals by resting either end of an iron spit in two very long (about sixteen-inch) pot or S hooks hung from the crane. This is a practice that fits in with the custom of building a cooking fire without andirons that was common to the settlers of certain sections of Pennsylvania, as mentioned in Chapter 2, The Cooking Fire.

A large fish was splinted with sticks and tied to these horizontal spits. A cut of meat or whole fowl was pierced through its cavity, or thickest part, and then skewered and tied to the spit to hold it in place while it roasted. One end of these spits was usually bent by the blacksmith to serve as a handle for turning the roasting food more easily.

A refinement of the standard spit design was the basket or cradle spit. Basket spits were simply modified, standard spits in which the spit's center was intersected by a large ovoid metal basket, or cage-like compartment. In this basket, the cook placed fragile-fleshed foods, such as fish, before the fire to roast. The basket simplified the process of attaching these foods to the spit by eliminating splinting and tying. They also helped to preserve the food's shape and appearance for serving, and prevented juices from escaping, since a basket spit did not pierce the skin or flesh of the roasting food.

While these simple, yet satisfactory methods (cord, plank, and spit) enabled the fireplace cook to roast her foods to perfection, and to ensure even cooking, they did require that she or someone else be in constant attendance to baste and turn the roasting food. Whenever possible the cook assigned her children to the task of sitting by the fire and patiently turning the roast, not an umpleasant job in the freezing winter months. In England, often poor children were paid a small sum to perform this job. They were called turnspits. When manpower was unavailable, sometimes even dogs were recruited to turn the spit. Specially trained for the task, these animals walked in a cage on a treadmill which activated a system of gears causing the spitted meat to rotate before the fire. Canine spits were first used in Tudor England and later brought to the Colonies.

But the best solution to this problem was the invention of mechanisms called jacks to turn the roasting food automatically. These jacks included the commonly used clock jack, the less frequently seen smoke jack, and the even rarer steam jack.

A smoke jack, interestingly enough, was designed by Leonardo da Vinci in the fifteenth century, but not introduced to the American hearth until the eighteenth century. Also called a chimney wheel because of its appearance and location, the smoke jack was installed in the chimney throat, where it utilized the updraft of hot air from the fire to turn its fan-shaped blades. The resultant windmill effect caused a series of connecting gears and chains to turn the spitted food, roasting it evenly without so much as a glance or prod from the cook.

In the late 1700's a steam jack was patented by John Bailey of New York City. In this unusual device, steam generated by the heat of the fire was harnessed to turn the roasting spit. But steam jacks were either impractical or didn't work very well, and few were manufactured.

The most commonly used jacks in the American fireplace were the clock jacks. These did not rely for their energy on the unpredictable pressure of the chimney's updraft or on the varying heat of the fire to produce a steady supply of steam. Developed during Charles II's reign as King of England, clock jacks, like the rarer jacks described above, appeared on the American hearth in the eighteenth century. In its simplest version, the clock jack utilized a tightly coiled clock spring mechanism to turn the roasting food. This jack resembled an ordinary wooden potato masher or bottle, and is sometimes referred to as a bottle jack. It was usually made of brass, and a long chain and hook hung from it to which the cook attached her roast. The masher or bottle-shaped case held the clock spring mechanism, which the cook wound with a key. As the spring mechanism unwound it caused the chain and the meat to revolve before the fire.

Another more complicated and perhaps earlier version of the clock jack was often called a gravity jack, since it translated the energy created by dropping a weight or weights to turn the roasting spit. It worked on a principle similiar to that of tall case clocks. The cook wound the weights of the gravity clock jack with a crank attached to a flywheel. As the weights slowly dropped, the energy released turned a series of gears, connected to a rope, a pulley, and finally to the spit.

By far the best all-around device developed for roasting during the fireplace cooking period was not the manual or automatic spit, but the reflector oven. These were similar to the reflector baking ovens described in the preceding chapter. The reflector roasting oven was a cylindrical shiny box on legs, with a large opening on one side to expose the roasting food to the fire. Not only was it lightweight, but it combined in a single unit all the best features of the other roasting implements. Incorporated in this ingenious device were an adjustable spit with skewers, dripping pan with spout, reflecting panels, a hinged door for checking the roast's progress and for basting it, handles for moving the oven, and in its most refined models, small hooks on the underside of its top edge from which the cook hung pieces of food to roast too small to be threaded on the central spit.

Unquestionably the *pièce de résistance* of fireplace roasting apparatus, the tin kitchen remains as impressive a device today as it was yesterday. It is still useful even in our generally smaller modern fireplaces that are often surrounded by carpeting and finished floors, where neatness and compactness are especially important. And while antique examples of this implement are rare and extremely expensive, reproductions can be ordered from many private tinsmiths and through the catalogs and museum shops of the larger restorations. Chapter 10, Sources for Equipping Your Cooking Hearth, lists a number of outlets for reflector roasting ovens.

In addition to the tin kitchen and the basic horizontal spit, many other specialty roasting devices were developed for fireplace cooking. One of these was the bird-roaster or oven. Essentially, this device was only a smaller, simpler tin kitchen. A small, free-standing, L-shaped piece of tin, the bird roaster was equipped with sharp hooks that protruded from the vertical, reflecting panel half of the shape. From these hooks the cook hung songbirds—a commonly consumed delicacy on the early American table—or other small pieces of meat that she wished to roast. The bottom, or horizontal, half of the oven served as a support and as a pan to catch the drippings from the roasting morsels.

Another roasting device, seen less frequently on the American hearth, was the English roasting frame. It resembled an instrument of torture more than a cooking tool. From a tall, vertical shaft of iron which stood on three legs protruded a series of sharp, dangerous spikes. On these spikes, the cook impaled the food she desired to roast, placing the frame in front of the fire's heat. Below the meat spikes, a circular ring of metal held a removable basin which caught the drippings.

Coffee roasters were another interesting group of devices which were developed for fireplace roasting. These roasters were of two general designs. In the first group, a long iron rod with a pointed end had a cylindrical metal compartment with a sliding or hinged door attached near the pointed end for holding raw coffee beans. To roast the beans, the cook held the roaster and twirled it as one would an umbrella, its pointed end on the hearth floor, near enough to the fire to heat the beans. The other general type of coffee roaster was a self-supporting unit. The coffee bean compartment in this unit rested on a special rack under which coals were placed. The cook turned a crank or handle attached to the end of the coffee bean container to rotate it for even roasting of the beans inside.

Yet another group of roasting accessories for the fireplace were popcorn and chestnut roasters. They both worked on the same basic principle, and are made much the same in design today as they were in early America. In most of these roasters, basket-like compartments made of wire or pierced metal held the kernels of corn or nuts. These were attached to long wooden or metal handles so that the cook could hold the basket at a comfortable distance from the fire or over its coals while the corn popped or the nuts roasted. A common mistake, by the way, made today when popping corn or roasting nuts in the fireplace, is to place the basket in the fire's flame. This practice tends to char and burn the corn and nuts before they have had a chance to pop or roast properly.

Techniques For Today

There are four methods of roasting food that we have found particularly suitable to today's fireplaces. For meat, these techniques are: hanging the roast or fowl by a length of butcher's twine; skewering the meat on a new horizontal spit (either one made expressly for fireplace use, or a barbecue spit modified for this purpose); roasting the meat in a reproduction tin kitchen; and planking, the best method for cooking fish. We have included planking in the roasting category since the cooking is performed before the fire.

The Hanging Cord

Roasting food by hanging it in front of the fire on a cord is an especially easy and inexpensive technique. It requires only a few yards of heavy cotton or butcher's twine from your butcher, or from a 5 & 10 or hardware store. Using about three yards of this material, truss or tie your meat or fowl in a secure package. Do not cut off the leftover piece of cord, but attach it to a nail in your fireplace mantel, to the damper handle, or even to the crane, adjusting the cord so that the roast hangs directly in front of the fire. Be sure to choose a tying place that allows the meat to fall fairly close to the fire (about five inches in front is desirable), and low enough so that it hangs directly in front of the tunnel formed by the log configuration of the cooking fire. This position will give the roast the full benefit of the fire's intensity. Next, place a dripping pan under the roast, and reflecting panels in front of it. Reflecting panels are optional, but are easily made in a few moments (see Chapter 1). Their use makes maximum use of the energy of the fire by reflecting its heat onto the side of the roast opposite the fire, and will cook your food rapidly and evenly.

As the meat roasts, occasionally prod it with a large meat fork. This will cause the cord to wind up, and, as it unwinds, to turn the roast, exposing all sides of it to the fire. (If you don't use reflecting panels, keeping the roast turning is especially important.) Also baste the meat with pan drippings whenever you think of it.

To ensure even cooking, and after the roast is about half done, turn it so that the uppermost part, which is generally somewhat cooler, now points down

Roasting a duck on a length of butcher's twine. Other foods, such as a chicken, goose, and leg of lamb can be roasted this way as well. Be sure to place a generous-sized pan under the cooking food to catch the drippings. (String is tied to nail in mantle.)

toward the hearth, where it is exposed to the fire's fullest intensity. The easiest way to accomplish this switch is to have a friend support the roasting food on a plate to relieve the considerable tension on the cord. Next, cut the slack cord at the point where it is joined to the roast and retie it to the trussing string on the other end of the roast. Then remove the plate and continue roasting until the food is done.

We usually determine doneness by inserting an instant meat thermometer when we anticipate that the meat is nearly cooked based on weight of the roast. But a conventional meat thermometer could be used as well, by inserting it before the roasting process commences. For smaller fowl—chicken, ducks, Cornish hens—we don't bother with a meat thermometer at all, since doneness can accurately be judged by cutting into a joint, twisting a leg, or any of the other regular methods of checking a fowl to detect whether or not it is cooked adequately. For turkeys, which are usually considerably larger than other roasting fowls, we make an exception to this rule, and recommend that you use a meat thermometer or purchase prepared roasting turkeys with the button that pops up when they are cooked. Some of the larger roasting chickens are now packaged with these handy indicators, as well.

The Roasting Spit

One of the most practical ways of roasting meat in your fireplace is on a horizontal spit. In the interest of economy a spit is most cheaply devised by having a blacksmith make a new one for you out of a length of square bar stock, and a pair of brackets or tripods to support it out of angle iron. The brackets should be designed so that the spit can be supported at different levels before the fire for temperature control. The spit's thickness should be selected to permit the modern "U" shaped rotisserie or barbecue skewers, with wing nuts for tightening them to the spit, readily found in hardware stores, to slide along its length. These skewers are the best gadgets we have found for holding meat on a spit. Although any competent and fairly imaginative blacksmith could fabricate such a combination for you, Jay Mickle, recommended under blacksmiths who do custom work in Chapter 10, Sources for Equipping Your Cooking Hearth, has developed a very satisfactory and reasonably priced model for us. His model (which he will make to order) is versatile and sturdy enough to roast either a hefty suckling pig or a dainty duck before the fire.

If you want to add an authentic period look and feel to your roasting activities, nothing is more impressive than good reproductions of old cooking andirons, spits and skewers. Most blacksmiths and other craftsmen listed in Chapter 10 will make handsome reproductions of these implements for you, although the expense will be considerably greater than that of the simpler spit and bracket arrangement just described. Also keep in mind that when using cooking andirons, you will have to lay your cooking fire directly on them, rather than on the fireplace floor.

To roast your meat on a spit, season it as your recipe directs, and if it is a fowl, truss it with cotton string or butcher's twine, as well. Then thread the spit through the thickest part of the meat, or poke it through the cavity of the fowl, and skewer it very securely in place so that when the spit is rotated, the meat turns along with it. Next, rest the spit on the brackets or cooking andirons so that the roast sits directly in front of the tunnel of the cooking fire. Here it receives the full benefit of the fire's heat. Place a dripping pan under the food and reflecting panels in front of it. Let the roast cook, occasionally basting and turning it, so that it browns nicely on all sides. Test for doneness with a meat thermometer, or by any of the other methods mentioned above in the discussion on roasting with a hanging cord.

To adjust the roasting temperature when cooking food on the improvised bracket supports, the cook has the options of either raising or lowering the spit in front of the fire, or of moving the brackets holding the spit closer to or further away from the fire.

The Tin Kitchen

The tin kitchen is in reality nothing more than an embellished spit with all of its accessories attached, and the procedure for roasting in it is exactly the same as

Suckling pig roasting on a spit before the fire. Oven liners make good reflecting panels when fastened together with screws. When used as shown they greatly improve the cooking efficiency of the fire.

the procedure for using an ordinary spit. With the tin kitchen, unlike the spit, temperature control can be achieved only by moving the entire oven closer to, or further away from, the fire. To maximize the oven's roasting potential, be sure to keep the interior reflecting surfaces bright and shiny. If you are using an old oven that has lost its shine, lining it with aluminum foil will recreate the original effect of the tin-coated surfaces.

The main advantage to using a tin kitchen over the simple spit is that this device is essentially spatterproof, since the cooking meat is shielded on three sides by the reflecting panels of the oven. This is an important consideration if your fireplace is located in a setting where spattered grease would be difficult or impossible to remove.

There are several drawbacks to using a tin kitchen, however. One is that its normal size limits the number of chickens, ducks, etc., that you can cook at once to approximately two. Also antique tin kitchens are exceedingly rare, and among the most expensive of the period roasting devices, and they are frequently found with some essential part missing or broken. Reproductions are available from a number of restorations and independent tinsmiths, but these copies are very expensive, as well.

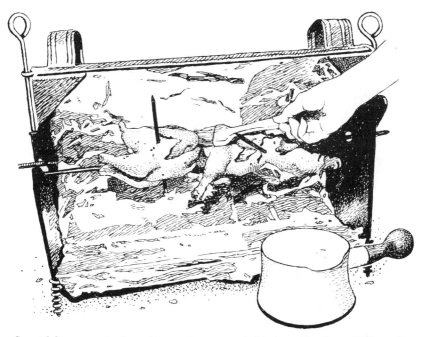

Cornish hens roasting in a nineteenth-century tin kitchen. Aluminum foil is used to line the oven to improve the reflecting ability of the worn metal.

Planking a Fish

Planking is a simple and inexpensive way of roasting a fish in your fireplace. The procedure requires little more than a flat, clean board of hardwood large enough to hold the fish you want to cook. If you don't have a piece of hardwood handy, a board of softwood covered with aluminum foil, shiny side up, will do. The foil keeps the softer wood from catching fire, which it will do more readily than the hardwoods, and prevents the food from picking up an unpleasant flavor caused by direct contact with the resins of many softwoods, especially pine.

To plank a whole fish, prepare it as your recipe directs, seasoning and stuffing it. Then place it on the wood roasting sheet and place fat rolls of aluminum foil, slightly thicker than the fish, along either side of it. (The purpose of the foil is to relieve the stress of the cord binding the fish to the board, and prevents it from cutting into the skin and flesh of the fish as it cooks.) Next, tie the fish to the plank by winding butcher's twine around it and the board, a number of times. Prop the fish up horizontally with a brick, log, or pot before the fire to roast. If it is stuffed, place the cavity opening up, an extra precaution against the filling's dripping out. When the fish is done on the side exposed to the fire, it should be flopped, or turned over, on the plank, so

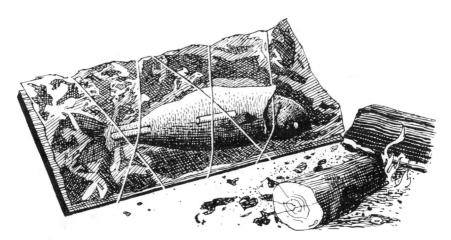

A whole fish can be planked, too. Instead of nailing it to the plank, tie it securely with sturdy string or butcher's twine. A stuffed fish is placed belly side up before the fire first to set the filling. It is also helpful to put a roll of foil or a dowel of wood (2 wooden spoons will do) next to each side of the fish to relieve the pressure from the string and prevent it from cutting into the soft flesh of the fish.

that both sides can cook evenly. To accomplish this, simply untie the string, turn the fish with spatulas, and replace the foil rolls and string. Continue to roast until the other side is cooked.

To test the fish for doneness, pierce its flesh with the tip of a sharp knife or the tines of a fork. The flesh should flake easily when it is cooked. To serve: remove the string and rolls of foil, and garnish the fish right on the plank with lemon wedges, sprigs of fresh parsley, and, if your board is large enough, the

Fish fillet nailed to plank roasting before the fire.

accompanying vegetables. Present the garnished fish to your guests and serve it right from this innovative platter.

To roast fish fillets on a plank, attach them to the board with nails instead of twine. Most any common nails will do. They should be clean, of medium thickness and at least 1 inch long. Place the fillets on the board, skin side down, and barely hammer the nails into the board through the edges of the fillets, so that they are easy to remove when the fish is cooked. Place nails all around the perimeter of the fish, spacing them about 1 1/2 inches apart. Then, prop the planked fillets vertically in front of the fire to roast until done. There is no need to turn or "flop" fillets during cooking, as recommended for a whole fish, since they are so thin, but one may want to baste them to keep them from drying out. It may also be necessary to shift the position of the board so that the upper and lower parts of the fillets cook evenly. Test for doneness in the same way as for a whole fish. When cooking is completed, carefully remove nails with pliers, and serve the fillets garnished on the board as suggested above for a whole planked fish.

It is a good idea to save the planking board, so you don't have to scrounge around for another the next time you wish to plank a fish.

Toasting, In Early America

As a cooking technique, toasting is much the same as roasting in that it uses the naked fire to cook food. The main differences between the two are the length of cooking time involved, and the foods generally cooked by this method. In general, toasting requires less cooking time than roasting, and it is a technique largely associated with bread or other baked goods, rather than with cuts of meat. Additionally, since toasting traditionally involves bread, drippings, which could cause the fire to smoke, are not produced during the cooking process. Hence, the cook is not limited when toasting to solely placing her food before the fire, as she is roasting. She can hold it over coals, or even over the burning fire, provided it's above the flames.

In early American fireplaces, food was either toasted by holding it in front of the fire or over its coals with a toasting fork, or by placing it in a fireplace toaster in front of the fire. Toasting forks were simply large two-pronged forks with long handles. Some of these oversized forks had short feet as well, so that they could sit on the hearth floor and toast food without the cook's help.

Regular fireplace toasters, also called down-hearth toasters, consisted of shallow wrought iron racks on short legs with a handle. They held one or two slices of bread before the fire. In the earliest fireplace toasters, the racks were stationary. To toast bread in these models, when one side of the bread is browned, the cook had to remove the slice and replace it, turning the un-toasted side towards the fire. An improvement was for the toasting rack to revolve, so that with a nudge from her fork the cook could turn the uncooked

Toasting bread slices in an antique toaster. Slices must be turned to permit even browning.

side of the toast towards the fire. And in the later fireplace toasters, very long handles were hinged where they joined the racks, so that the cook did not even have to bend down to turn the roast—a twist of her wrist accomplished this maneuver instead.

Fireplace toasters were also among the most attractive of all the open-hearth cooking implements. The bars forming their wrought iron racks were often twisted and bent into ornate and delicate shapes, which left a brand or shadow on the toasted bread.

While toasting seems so simple and straightforward a process to us today, historically the rationale and procedure for toasting in America's cooking fireplaces was discussed at length, almost to the point of absurdity by some early cooks. Here is an example of these excesses from *The Boston Cook Book of 1883:*

> Bread is toasted . . . before the fire to extract the moisture and make it more palatable and disgestible. If the slices be cut thick and carelessly exposed to a blazing fire, the outside is blackened and made into charcoal before the heat can reach the inside; the moisture is only heated, not evaporated, making the inside doughy . . . The correct way is to have the bread stale, and cut into thin uniform slices about one quarter of an inch thick.
>
> For toasting the bread . . . The fire should be clear, red (not blazing) coals. If you require only one or two slices, a toasting-fork will answer; but if a larger quantity be needed, there is nothing better than a double broiler.

To toast cheese and other thick foods that will not fit in your fireplace toaster, either toast them on a long-handled kitchen fork or rest them on a gridiron before the fire. Raclette is pictured here melting before the fire. The foil covering the gridiron catches cheese that melts before diners can catch it.

Bread properly dried and toasted is changed from the nature of dough, which always has a tendency to sour on the stomach, into pure wheat farina. It is not so scorched as to turn the butter into oil, but absorbs the butter; the butter and farina being easily separated, are quickly acted upon by the gastric fluid. Many persons prefer toast that is soft inside, but it should never be served to sick people in that manner.

Techniques for Today: The Toasting Fork, Fireplace Toaster, and Double Broiler

Toasting in one's fireplace is accomplished in much the same way today, as it was in the eighteenth century. In place of an antique toasting fork one can use a long barbecue fork with a wooden handle for toasting bread, muffins, and even marshmallows before the fire. Hold the fork so that the food to be toasted sits before the fire or over its coals, but never in its flames.

If you have an authentic fireplace toaster, the kind with a rack and feet, place it on the hearth in front of the fire to toast your bread. Antique examples of this implement are still fairly plentiful, but they do command high prices. Reproductions, which are generally cheaper and just as attractive as the originals, are a favorite commission of contemporary blacksmiths, since they give them a chance to display a variety of their skills. A list of craftsmen from whom one can order a toaster can be found in Chapter 10, Sources for Equipping Your Cooking Hearth.

Another way to broil your hot dogs, hamburgers, etc. is to place them in an ordinary two-sided barbecue grill with handles and prop before the fire. Again, foil is used to keep hearth clean and improve reflected heat.

Slices of bread, split muffins, and even bagels can also be toasted in the ordinary flat hinged grills sold for cooking hotdogs and hamburgers on your barbecue. These grills closely approximate the "double broilers" mentioned in *The Boston Cook Book of 1883*. They will hold about four slices of bread at one time—at least twice the capacity of the wrought iron fireplace toasters and the toasting forks. The easiest way to toast bread slices in these grills is to prop them up before the fire with a log, pot, or brick at a fairly steep angle. When one side of the food is browned, turn the grill to toast the other side. These grills can also be held over a bed of coals to toast their contents, but this is more work for the cook.

Broiling in Early America

Unlike broiling in today's ovens, broiling on the American hearth was performed over the heat source—a bed of glowing coals—rather than under it—exactly the same technique that we use in our modern barbecue grills. But in contrast with the popularity barbecuing enjoys, broiling—or grilling, as it was sometimes called—was not a favored food preparation technique in early America. Fireplace cooks disliked the smoky flavor imparted to the food by the drippings of the cooking meat as they fell on the glowing coals. Also for broiled meat to be enjoyable, it had to be tender—a quality early American cooks were not accustomed to in their cuts of meat. The average housewife or cook had wild game or old, sinewy domestic animals as her source of meat. Neither was naturally tender, and broiling did nothing to improve this quality.

When meat was broiled at the early American hearth, the cook often parboiled it first. Parboiling ensured that the meat would be thoroughly cooked when it was removed from the grill, since broiling was described, and is in practice, a quick method of cooking foods. Parboiling chicken parts before broiling them was a common practice, and one that was recommended by Eliza Leslie. She observed that if one did not cook the thicker pieces of chicken, such as the thigh and leg, before broiling, they had a tendency to become charred on the outside while the inside remained raw.

The implements used for broiling food on the early American hearth were gridirons and broilers. The gridirons resembled square grills raised up from the hearth by short legs. A handle extended from one end. The cook placed these grills over a bed of coals to provide the heat necessary for broiling her food, and placed her meat directly on its well-greased bars. She let the underside of the steak (or other food) cook until done on this side and then poured any juices accumulated on its surface into a nearby dish and reserved them for later use. She then turned the food to cook its reverse side.

More elaborate gridirons were produced by some imaginative blacksmiths. These gridirons had slightly taller front legs and grooves or channels in the upper surfaces of the flat bars that made up the grilling area. As the meat cooked, its juices trickled down these grooves into a narrow trough at the lower end of the gridiron, and were poured off by the cook. These natural cooking juices were either served with the meat *au naturel,* as is, or were thickened to make a gravy for it.

Gridiron broiling on an antique (right) and on a new inexpensive reproduction from the Pottery Barn (left). Note coals are placed on foil to improve their heating ability and to keep the hearth clean and grease-free.

The other group of implements commonly used for broiling were themselves called broilers. The cooking area on these was usually round, and like the gridirons, they had a handle and short legs to raise the grilling area above a bed of coals. Many broilers had attractive wavy bars across their grilling surfaces instead of the ordinary straight ones standard on the gridiron. Apart from supporting the meat in style, and leaving attractive marks on the cooked food, this design variation had no apparent function. On some broilers, the circular grilling surface turned on its tripod-like legs, presumably allowing the cook to regulate the broiling temperature or to check her meat for doneness with ease. In another ingenious design, the broiler's bars had channels in them and were tilted slightly downward towards the center of the circular implement. As the meat cooked, its juices dripped down these channels, pooling into a central well, which then directed them still further into a handle, which doubled as a trough, and had a final, larger well in its end. Aside from these variations, the cook proceeded with her cooking on a broiler as she would have with a gridiron.

Techniques for Today: The Gridiron or Broiler and Fish Grill

Except for a few refinements, broiling is most easily performed in modern fireplaces in much the same way today as it was yesterday. The most important of these variations is to be sure to cover your hearth cooking area with several thicknesses of aluminum foil before you begin your broiling. This step will not only save you a messy clean-up job when your cooking is completed, but will prevent grease from accumulating on your hearth and causing a potentially hazardous fire.

The implements best suited for fireplace broiling today are antique gridirons and broilers, or copies of them, and the basket fish grills with feet on top and bottom, commonly sold in gourmet kitchen equipment stores for barbecue use. The Bridge Kitchenware Corporation, Inc., is an excellent source for these grills. They are listed in Chapter 10, Sources for Equipping Your Cooking Hearth.

To broil in your fireplace, choose an area for cooking, if space permits, that is away from your central fire. Cover the hearth floor here with several thicknesses of heavy-duty aluminum foil, cutting the sheets slightly larger than the size of your broiling implement. Next season your meat, or prepare it as your recipe directs, and place it on the gridiron or broiler, or in the fish grill. It is helpful to lightly oil the cooking bars of your grilling implement first, to prevent the food from sticking to these surfaces as it cooks. Then, when the fire has developed a healthy supply of red hot coals, begin cooking. First shovel a generous amount of the coals onto the foil, and spread them out so

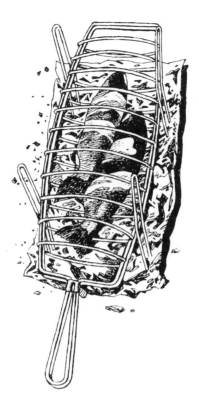

*A good way to broil trout is in a basket fish grill made today for barbecue use.
Placing foil on the hearth under the coals will keep the hearth grease-free and
make clean-up easier. Other fish, as well as small steaks and lamb chops can
also be cooked this way.*

that they cover an area equal to the whole grilling area of your implement, or
to the underside of your food. Place the gridiron, broiler, or fish grill over
these coals and let the food cook on one side until done to your liking. Then, if
the food is cooking on a gridiron or broiler, turn it with a meat fork. (Before
you do this, pour off any accumulated surface juices into a side dish.) To turn
the food cooking in a fish grill, simply turn the whole device over so that it is
now resting on its top legs, instead of its bottom ones.

It should not be necessary to refresh the coals for broiling, as they usually
give off enough heat for twenty to thirty minutes of cooking, an adequate
length of time to broil most foods. If you find that you do need to add more
coals to complete your cooking, the best way to do this is to remove the gridiron
or other implement from the foil cooking area before refreshing the coals. This
will prevent any ashes that may be disturbed from getting onto your food.

If your fireplace is too small to permit broiling in a location other than over the central fire, just lay your cooking fire on layers of foil, and let it die down to a bed of glowing coals, then broil right there. To clean up your fireplace: after dinner, when the coals are cold, simply fold up the foil, coals and all, and discard the whole package.

While hamburgers, steaks, and lamb chops are favorite broiled fireplace fare, fish cooked over the coals is a special culinary treat. This is where fireplace broiling strikes its tastiest note. And, as a final tip on broiling in your fireplace, fish grills are very handy for broiling small filet steaks, and chicken parts, as well as fish, and other small pieces of meat.

Browning Off: The Salamander and Ember Tongs

Since broiling was accomplished in the fireplace by placing food over the coals, the practice of running a casserole or other food under the broiler as we do today to give its surface a lovely, golden brown crust or glaze, was not possible. Instead, to brown off the tops of her food, the early cook brought the heat of the fire over it. For this purpose she frequently used an implement known as a salamander (Hannah Glasse calls it an "iron for browning off" in her book.) A salamander consisted of a circular metal disc, about one inch thick, which was attached to a long handle. The cook buried the disc end of the salamander in the coals until it was red hot and then held it close to the top of a pie pastry or the surfaces of any other foods that she wished to finish with a golden brown

Browning off tops of foods can easily be accomplished by holding a hot coal near their cooked surfaces. Here ember tongs are used to grip the coal, but ordinary kitchen or barbecue tongs, provided they are metal, will work just as well.

"Browning off" with an ash shovel which has been preheated in the glowing coals.

color. The unusual name for the implement is derived from the mythical salamander, an animal which had the power to endure fire. If the cook did not own a salamander, she "browned off" her foods by passing red hot coals over them, grasping the coals with a pair of ember or pipe tongs.

Both of these methods of browning off are recommended to the modern fireplace cook, in addition to the following substitutions. In place of a salamander, an iron peel could be heated in the coals of the fire and held over the food. But since the spade end of a peel is much thinner than that of the traditional salamander, it will not hold as much heat, or retain it for as long a period of time, as the salamander will. Or in lieu of either the antique salamander or peel, a *crème brûlée* iron, sold through gourmet equipment stores and catalogs, works on the same principle as the salamander. Normally used for caramelizing the sugar topping on your *crème brûlée*, the implement can be used at your fireplace for finishing your pie crusts and casseroles. And, if ember or pipe tongs are not available, ordinary fireplace or barbecue tongs will work just as well for manipulating the hot coals.

5

Boiling, Simmering, Steaming, and Related Techniques

rimming kettles of fragrant soups and stews bubbling on the hearth are surely among the first images to flash to one's mind when thinking of fireplace cookery. And undoubtedly the English ancestry of this country's earliest settlers and the cuisine they brought with them—one which favored boiling and simmering foods, even to this day—is largely responsible for these lingering impressions. But as one begins to examine life in early America it becomes quickly apparent how well adapted a simmering pot of food was to our ancestor's way of life, and why boiling and steaming foods have continued to thrive in our cooking.

In Early America

The first American homemakers had to have been the original harried housewives. Among the many duties for which the colonial homemaker was responsible, cooking was just another chore, and a minor one, at that. Her duties were endless, and even the most basic items had to be prepared or fabricated by hand. She oversaw the family vegetable garden, preserved food for winter, spun thread and wove it into cloth garments, and blankets, made soap and candles, and raised her children. And she did not even have the benefit of running water, plumbing, or the numerous other simple aids we now regard as necessities.

With this overwhelming workload, time was a very precious commodity, and ease and speed of food preparation became crucial. Putting whatever food was available (thin'ins from the garden, or a freshly caught rabbit) into a large pot with water, and placing it over the fire was a most expedient way to prepare lunch and dinner. Among the easiest ways to cook foods, boiling and simmering offered many other advantages for the household.

Of all the food preparation techniques, a simmering pot also required the least attention from the cook. The kettle's contents were first brought to a boil, and any foam carefully skimmed off as it rose to the surface. The pot was then covered and left to simmer slowly on the back of the hearth, for hours, and sometimes even for days, as in the preparation of samp porridge. An Indian goulash eaten by the settlers, this consisted of a combination of cornmeal, meat, and vegetables. Samp porridge was cooked for at least three days, and was considered done when the mixture was so thick it could be removed from the pot in a solid chunk!

With the exception of an occasional stir, or the addition of more water to keep the pot from boiling dry, the simmering kettle required no other attention from the cook. While one did have to remember to keep the fire going, length of cooking time was not a major concern for these simple meals. Experience taught housewives that the soup or stew always tasted better on the second day, after the flavors of the different ingredients had had a chance to "marry."

The combination of boiling and slow simmering was also needed to tenderize the generally tough pieces of meat the cook had at her disposal. Meat, especially beef, in early America did not have the finely marbled, tender qualities we are so accustomed to today. Cattle were not raised for slaughter, and the practice of tenderizing meat by grinding or chopping it into hamburgers and adding fat, did not become popular until the late nineteenth or early twentieth century. Instead, as we have seen, the fireplace cook depended on infrequently slaughtered domestic livestock or wild game for the meat in her meals, and both were notoriously tough!

In the earliest years of America's settlement, domestic animals were very costly and scarce, since they had to be imported from England and Europe. As a result, cows, chickens, goats, and sheep were primarily raised for their milk, eggs, and wool, or to pull the farmer's plow. A milk cow, for example, cost $1,400 in 1620. And although by 1700 its price had dropped to $250, it was still a very valuable possession, considering that most rural housewives spent, on the average, $20 a year for their flour, sugar, and all other household staples combined. So when these animals finally did reach the cooking pot, they had more than outlived their usefulness, and certainly their tenderness.

One frequently comes across recipes in old cookbooks specifically for preparing the meat of animals that were past their prime. One such recipe, entitled "Soup of Any Kind of Old Fowl, The only way in which they are eatable," is found in identical versions in *The Virginia Housewife*, by Mrs. Mary Randolph, and in *The Frugal Colonial Housewife*, by Susannah Carter. A recipe you're not likely to come across in cookbooks today, it directs the reader to first "Put the fowls in a coop and feed them moderately for a fortnight;"

Wild game, the cook's most regular source of meat, was tough, too. Possum, squirrel, rabbit, deer, bear, and moose were some of the plentiful native creatures that were most often found in the cook's pot, and they, too, needed hours of slow simmering to make them edible.

Even for roasting, parboiling the meat first was a technique many cooks relied upon to ensure a tender roast. While many of the more sophisticated cooks of the period frowned on this practice, as they felt it diminished the flavor of the meat, which surely it did, the meat probably required it.

Neither could homemakers of the past also be particular about the cuts of meat they cooked. They were grateful for whatever their husband or son was lucky enough to snare or shoot on any day to fill their cookpot.

This rather unpredictable method of obtaining meat also made these cooks quite frugal. Not sure of when the next rabbit or wild turkey would be theirs, they were very conscious of waste, and when confronted with a whole animal (the usual situation) were challenged to prepare every part of it, from horns to hooves, in a tasty fashion. Again, boiling and slow simmering were the methods the cook utilized to transform the less tender and more unusual cuts of meat into palatable and often delicious meals.

Ironically today's emphasis on broiling and roasting, and the pressure for fast meal preparation, has practically eliminated the preparation of these tougher but very tasty parts of an animal's anatomy from our diet in favor of the more speedily-cooked and more reliably tender, but definitely less flavorful, portions.

Another factor which popularized boiling and slow simmering as a method of food preparation was the Colonial way of life. The hard-working, rural farm existence of many early American families discouraged them from eating meals together at set times, as we do today. Sundays and holidays were an exception to this practice, but on most days, farm chores came first, and family members were usually too busy even to sit in the household's sole chair when dining. When they finally did stop to eat, meals were often hastily consumed standing before the hearth or board (the common name for the improvised or crude table) whenever one felt hungry and had a spare moment. So an ever-ready pot of dinner was a convenience for the diner, as well as for the cook.

And lastly, the softened nature of boiled and simmered foods probably made them widely preferred because of the generally poor condition of early American teeth. Inadequate diet and lack of care took their toll on the teeth of our ancestors. Pregnancy was especially hard on the women's teeth, and the adage, "A tooth (lost) for every child," was particularly applicable then. Throughout the general population teeth were weakened and/or missing entirely, too. And although everyone has heard of George Washington's famous wooden dentures, it is unlikely that the poorer members of society, or even the middle class, could have afforded such luxuries. As a consequence, the population was not able to manage food that required strenuous biting or chewing. Meals boiled and simmered until the meat was reduced to rags were easy for them to digest with little or no effort.

In view of these myriad factors, it is easy to understand why the simmering cookpot became a permanent fixture on every hearth and why the all-purpose iron pot used to produce these boiled and simmered meals was considered the most basic fireplace cooking implement. Indeed, in the seventeenth century, it was not infrequently the only pot a homemaker owned.

Commonly called a cooking kettle, or today a gypsy kettle, the early pots used to produce these boiled meats were usually cast of iron. They were rounded in shape with three short stubby feet, and were produced in a variety of sizes from very small to enormous. Most had handles which were attached, while others only had small loops on each side from which an adjustable handle which looked like big calipers was hooked. The feet raised the bottom of the pot above the fireplace floor so coals could be placed under it for cooking purposes. They also gave it stability when it was simply sitting on the hearth floor or other flat surface for serving or storing. The handle was used, of course, for lifting or moving the pot, but most importantly for hanging it over the fire from the crane or lugpole, its usual cooking position.

While the simple iron kettle was most popular, the basic version was sometimes improved with an enamel lining. This lining made the pots easier to keep clean and permitted certain foods to be cooked in them without the iron interacting with their flavor or color. Few examples of the lined kettles have survived with their linings intact or in usable condition.

Other metals were also used to make the common boiling vessel. Some of the largest and most beautiful examples we have seen have been made of copper. These were used outdoors for rendering pork fat, boiling down maple syrup, washing clothes, or making apple butter. These copper pots were much lighter than their iron versions, and were also more attractive, but they were not designed with feet, probably because copper feet would not have supported the weight of the full kettle. Instead, the bottoms of copper pots were usually flat and only their handles were made of a sturdier metal, such as iron. In place of feet or a handle, some of the largest copper kettles sat in their own circular iron frames or tripods over the fire. These frequently had rounded bottoms, which made them resemble giant mixing bowls. Inside the home, the smaller copper pots were designed to either hang from the crane or to rest on trivets, their usual "cooking" positions.

Occasionally cooking kettles were made of brass and even silver. A reference to silver kettles is made by Hannah Glasse in her eighteenth-century cookbook, *The Art of Cookery Made Plain and Easy.*

In addition to the general category of cooking kettles, early American kitchens were frequently equipped with a smaller, rounded-bottom pot which served the same purpose as our modern saucepan. Called posnets or skillets, these cousins of the cook's kettle were made of cast or wrought iron and were designed to sit over the coals on their short spindly legs. They were used for stewing small amounts of food, for making sauces, and generally for the same cooking needs as the large cook's kettle. Posnets, however, were called into play when smaller amounts of food were to be prepared.

In the seventeenth and eighteenth centuries, the dinner or luncheon meals prepared in these pots were broadly referred to as pottage. Roughly a cross between a soup and a stew, pottage was made from literally anything on hand. Vegetables, herbs, seasoning, and meat were all cut into small pieces and tossed into the cook's kettle with enough water to cover the ingredients. Generally assembled first thing in the morning, the combination was left to simmer slowly until mealtime.

In times of plenty, marvelous new recipes might result from the marriage of the unfamiliar native foods the settlers learned to enjoy, such as corn, and the usual combinations and substitutions of their own cooking heritages. All-American favorites, many of which were originally based on Indian dishes, such as Brunswick stew, clam chowder, and succotash, evolved this way.

Even under less bountiful circumstances, the kettle could produce surprisingly delicious results. Philadelphia pepper pot, a truly original American recipe, resulted from this imaginative "cook-what-you-have" approach. The soup was the inspiration of General George Washington's chef. The story is told that George Washington asked his camp cook to fix a special dinner to raise the morale of his haggard and hungry troops. The chef, undaunted by the limited supplies in his larder—tripe and generous supply of peppercorns—cooked them together in the kettle with water and produced a wonderful soup which all enjoyed and which they named in honor of the chef's inventiveness, after the city of his birth.

In winter, especially during its latter months, pottage could be as meager as flour soup, made from only milk and browned flour—a dish probably most commonly served during the last months of winter, from March until the first spring growth appeared, when food supplies were at their lowest. The colonists called this period "starving time," since it was reminiscent of the first winters of colonization when many did die of starvation.

Breakfast porridge was also a common food prepared in the big iron pot. Often mixed after the supper meal had emptied the contents of the pot, the porridge was left in the waning embers of the fire to cook slowly overnight in readiness for the next morning's meal. Porridge could also be cooked or reheated for several days, as in the Mother Goose rhyme: "Pease-porridge in the pot, nine days old."

Another product of the kettle was pocket or portable soup, our forefathers' version of the bouillon cube. Pocket soup came yesterday, as it does today, in two flavors: brown, beef-based; and white, chicken-based. The preparation of each was similar and required a lengthy and complicated reduction of the meat (which determined its color and flavor), vegetables, and water. Salt was omitted and added later when the cubes were reconstituted in water to use as a soup base, or to enrich sauces. An especially detailed and excellent description of how the early American housewife made these "soup concentrates" is given in *The Frugal Colonial Housewife*, by Susannah Carter.

Pocket soup was frequently carried on long trips by travelers and hunters, since it was so readily portable in one's pocket—hence its name. They would either let a cube of this soup melt in their mouths for nourishment when on the go, or, when time permitted, would drop one in boiling water at their campsite. With the addition of dried beans or corn, it made a very satisfying meal.

And, last but not least, the kettle was famous for its boiled dumplings and puddings. They came in great variety, and among them was the still familiar Indian and festive plum puddings, as well as an exotic pigeon pudding. While they haven't survived the swings in taste and current style in cuisine as well as soups and stews, boiled puddings were immensely popular and a staple of the early American diet.

The general procedure for their preparation was to wrap the pudding or dumpling mixture (a typical recipe called for fruit, eggs, flour, milk, and spices) in a thick pudding cloth that was first scalded in boiling water and then dredged in flour. To facilitate its filling and tying, the cloth was placed in a deep bowl so its sides could be easily drawn up around the soft mixture. The cloth was then filled and tied firmly, with plenty of room allowed for the pudding to swell as it cooked. The tying place was pasted with a small lump of moistened flour, an extra measure to keep the boiling water out. To quote Eliza Leslie, "If any water gets into the pudding it will be spoiled."

The pudding package was then lowered into a kettle filled with boiling water. A lid was placed on the pot, and it was left to cook for anywhere from two hours for a smallish meat dumpling to six for a large plum pudding. The pudding or dumpling was turned occasionally as it boiled to ensure even cooking.

Sometimes, instead of immersing her puddings in boiling water, the cook suspended them in the steam over a pot of soup to cook. Cooked by this method they could be more accurately called "steamed" rather than "boiled" puddings. Another variation was to place the pudding mixture in a simple metal can or a decorative pottery mold, if the cook was lucky enough to own one. These containers gave the cooked pudding a more attractive appearance than the free-form shape which resulted from the use of the pudding cloth.

Cooks were careful to keep the water in which the pudding cooked boiling at all times, and to replenish the pot, as it boiled away, with boiling water only. The introduction of cold water would have slowed down the cooking action in the pot and caused the finished pudding to be hard and heavy. A filled, hot teakettle was kept on the hearth for this purpose.

Puddings were served hot, and were not removed from the cooking pot until moments before they were to be served. Their generally bland flavor was usually enhanced at the table with a wine or cream sauce or a simple topping of sugar (or molasses), butter, and cinnamon. Leftover pudding was served the next day, sliced and fried.

Puddings and dumplings can be prepared much in the same manner today as they were yesterday. And while the cloth bag method just described can be copied with a fair amount of success, a modification of this technique that we feel is easier to execute and produces results more in keeping with contemporary tastes is given in the Techniques for Today section of this chapter, which follows.

The kettle was also capable of cooking two foods at once, a real energy- and time-saver, especially if you only had one pot! To accomplish this, the pudding was either cooked in the steam over a soup or other hot kettle, as described earlier in this chapter, or, if the cook was in a hurry to speed up the cooking process, she lowered the pudding right into the kettle's contents. Cooks who practiced this last technique claimed that the foods did not exchange flavors as they cooked together—or perhaps, if they did, it didn't bother them. This is a remarkable claim which we haven't verified in our fireplace cooking sessions! But an interesting observation on this unusual cooking practice has been suggested by Waverly Root and Richard de Rochemont in their excellent book, *Eating In America, A History*, published by William Morrow and Company. They propose that these mixed-food cooking habits have been in part responsible for Americans being unable to recognize fine shadings of taste, a failing we are frequently accused of today.

Beginning in the mid-eighteenth century, foods prepared in the all-purpose American cook-pot became much more sophisticated. Instead of just cutting meat into small pieces and tossing it into the kettle with whatever else was available, more attention was given to the final appearance and texture of the boiled dinners. A practice known as collaring, in which a joint was boned, rolled, and tied, became popular. Collaring meat prevented it from losing its shape or from falling apart in the lengthy boiling process. As a result, the boiled dinner could be neatly sliced after it was cooked and attractively presented at the table. Vegetables were still added to the boiling pot, but not until the meat was nearing completion, so that they would not become overcooked. Distinctions were also made between soups, stews, and ragouts. And one-dish meals were no longer referred to as pottage.

Recipes in early cookbooks that specified boiling and its related techniques—simmering, steaming, poaching, braising, and stewing—were plentiful, varied, and interesting. And directions for preparing almost every category of food, from puddings and breads to meat, fish, fowl, and vegetables, using one of these techniques, were included in all the early recipe collections. This is an indication of how much more popular boiling and its related techniques were yesterday than they are today.

In 1770, Martha Bradley summarized the principle of boiling food rather succinctly for her readers, we feel. "Boiling," she wrote, is the Dressing (of) Things by means of Water, as Roasting does it by the naked Fire. . . ."

And Amelia Simmons offered the following rules to be observed when cooking food in this manner:

> The First necessary caution is that your pots and covers are always kept clean—
> be careful that your pot is constantly boiling, by this means you may determine

with precision the time necessary to accomplish any dish you may wish to prepare in this way. Put fresh meat into boiling water, and salt into cold. Never croud your pot with meat, but leave sufficient room for a plenty of water. Allow a quarter of an hour to every pound of meat.

While these directions from the past for boiling may seem curious, this method of cooking food, and its related techniques—simmering, steaming, poaching, and braising—are still performed in much the same way today as they were yesterday. With a few modifications on the procedures used by the early American housewife, here is how to accomplish these techniques in your fireplace.

Techniques for Today

To boil, simmer, steam, braise, and poach, or in general to "dress food with water" in your fireplace, your most important implement will be a rather generous-sized pot with a lid. While we acknowledge that all these simple techniques can be executed in almost any size and shape vessel that is fireproof and holds water (some American Indians used freshly killed buffalo stomachs for this purpose), the large iron cook's kettle of yesterday was, and still is, the best implement for performing these tasks at the kitchen hearth.

The Cook's Kettle or Gypsy Kettle, and the Posnet

The original iron cook's kettle described earlier in this chapter is well suited to all of these cooking techniques, since it was intended expressly for these uses in a fireplace. When cooking, the kettle either hangs over the fire securely from an S hook on the crane, or from an adjustable trammel anchored in the chimney throat, or it rests comfortably over coals on the hearth. In addition, an antique kettle, which will lend an authentic air to your cooking activities, can most likely be found for a fairly reasonable price at a local antique shop, or even at a flea market. They were plentifully produced and were virtually indestructible, so many of them have survived undisturbed to this day. If you prefer a new kettle, good reproductions of the original cook's kettle are also being cast today. One such source is Iron Craft, a New Hampshire forge, listed in Chapter 10, Sources for Equipping Your Cooking Hearth. They produce good copies of this implement, fairly inexpensively, and in various sizes.

The only drawback to the traditional cook's kettle is that it was not originally designed and produced with its own lid. If some kettles did come outfitted with lids, this piece has long since disappeared. And for many of the following cooking techniques, especially steaming, a closely fitting lid is most desirable. This accessory is also generally handy for keeping straying embers and ashes out of the soup or to step up the heating process. To improvise or make a new lid for an old cooking pot, either borrow a lid from one of your kitchen pots or make a new one out of wood. Wooden lids are commonly in use with iron kettles of antique design at Plimoth Plantation. A word of precaution when using a lid from another pot: We have found that if the lid fits too snugly, there is a tendency for it to be sucked into the pot as the old iron expands from exposure to the fire's heat, causing a loud explosive sound and spattering the contents of the kettle. Selecting a lid that is slightly larger than seems necessary will avoid this problem, as will the use of a wooden lid, since the wood will expand from contact with the rising steam from the kettle, precluding the possibility of its falling into the soup.

The most common cooking position of these kettles, and the most versatile, is suspended over the fire from a crane by an S hook. To adjust the temperature of the kettle on the crane, the cook has three basic options. First she can slide the S hook holding the kettle along the crane, which will place the pot further away from or closer to the fire. Second, she can use a shorter or longer pothook to raise or lower the kettle. And third, she can swing the crane like a gate to almost any location in front of the fire and even out into the room. This last position is recommended for filling the pot, skimming its surface, testing or sampling the food in it, or serving its contents, since it is safest and easiest for the cook, and doesn't require that she lean over the hot fire to reach the kettle.

If your fireplace is not equipped with a crane, the second-best way of heating the kettle is to hang it over the fire from an adjustable trammel hung in the chimney throat. A trammel does not offer as many possibilities as does the crane for controlling the cooking temperature or the position of the pot, but this device does allow the cook to raise or lower her pot over the fire. Yet another alternative for heating the kettle is to place it on the hearth near the fire and to shovel a generous amount of coals under it. This last option is a great deal of work, requiring a plentiful supply of coals, frequent fire-tending, and almost constant surveillance of the pot by the cook to maintain a steady cooking temperature.

Having just outlined the basics of the use of the kettle with the cooking fire, we will describe how to execute the techniques of boiling, simmering, braising, steaming, and poaching in it at your hearth.

To boil in the kettle, it must be placed in the hottest position, or directly (about six to eight inches) above the flames of a small, but brisk and well-established fire. Boiling, as all cooks know, is characterized by lots of steam rising from the pot and large bubbles rapidly breaking the surface of the liquid. This action causes a walloping motion, which early American cooks used as a temperature measurement when cooking. They counted the frequency of the wallops to get an indication of how hot the liquid was, and therefore how long to cook the food immersed in it.

After a time, depending on the fire's intensity, the proximity of your pot to it, and the amount of food and liquid in your pot, its contents will reach a boil. There is a common saying that "a watched pot never boils," but the use of a lid will help matters along considerably.

Simmering, which is directly related to boiling, is cooking liquids at a temperature just below the boiling point. This temperature is reached when many tiny bubbles rise to the surface of the pot. Simmering obviously requires less heat than boiling, but it is accomplished in the same way. To simmer foods, place the kettle in the hottest position at your hearth—or on the crane directly over the fire—and cover it with a lid. When the liquid reaches the simmering point, maintain this temperature by moving the pot further away from the fire, either by sliding the S hook along the crane, swinging the crane further away from the fire, adjusting the trammel, or in any of the other ways outlined earlier of moving the pot away from the fire and thus adjusting its temperature.

While these are basically foolproof and self-explanatory techniques, a few specific rules governing boiling and simmering foods, which early American cooks adhered to and which still hold true today, follow.

When one is preparing a broth or stock, the meat and vegetables should be put into a cold pot with cold water and the ingredients slowly heated together. When the meat is to be the end product, it should be added to the pot after the water has reached the boiling point. And, as Eliza Leslie observed, " . . . if the fire is too great, and the soup boils too fast, the meat will become hard and tough, and will not give off its juices."

To boil a twentieth-century pudding in the cook's kettle, use an empty one-pound coffee can as a mold and grease the inside. Place your pudding mixture or other recipe batter in the can. Some breads can also be prepared in this manner. An example is the brown bread recipe in Chapter 8. The uncooked ingredients should only fill one-half to two-thirds of the can, in order to allow for expansion. Cover the can with a double thickness of waxed paper or aluminum foil, and secure the cover with string. Place the can (covered end up) on a trivet or rack in a large kettle and fill with enough boiling water to come halfway up the sides of the mold. Cover the kettle and boil until the pudding is done.

The kettle should be checked occasionally as the cooking proceeds and more boiling water should be added, if needed, to maintain the original water level. Add only boiling water to the kettle! (A teakettle on the hearth is a good, constant, source for hot water.) After the cooking is completed, the pudding should be removed from the can while still hot, sliced, and served warm, traditionally with a sauce or other topping.

Another less frequently executed but nonetheless interesting technique, related to "dressing food with water," and which can also be performed in the cook's kettle, is braising. Braising is the cooking of foods in a small amount of liquid, such as broth, wine, or water. To braise food in the kettle, first preheat the empty pot by hanging it over the fire—from the crane is best. Then sear your chicken or other meat in it in a small amount of butter or oil. Carefully rotate the food as it browns, being careful not to pierce its surface or skin, releasing its juices. After the meat is nicely colored on all sides, add a small amount of the braising liquid to the pot, together with herbs, seasonings, vegetables, or whatever ingredients your specific recipe calls for. Cover the pot and lower the cooking temperature by sliding the kettle along the crane away from the fire, by swinging the crane forward, or by any other appropriate means of temperature adjustment. Continue cooking at this lower temperature until the food is done, adding more of the braising liquid to the pot if it should become dry.

Steaming is another easy technique which is at home in the versatile kettle. To steam foods in it, place the pot in the hottest position on the hearth—suspended over the fire from the crane is again best—and fill it a quarter of the way up from the bottom with water. Cover and bring the water to a boil, and then place the food to be cooked in a basket or on a rack, inside the kettle, and support it in the steam over the hot water to cook. Steam the food until done, adding additional boiling water as needed to complete the cooking. Be sure to add only boiling water to the kettle, as the introduction of cold or even warm water could stop, or reduce, the steaming action and ruin your dish. Again, a teakettle is handy as a supply of boiling water at your hearth.

Poaching foods (eggs and fish are commonly associated with this technique) is another method of cooking food in water that lends itself readily to the cook's kettle. Although specially designed fish-poachers with handles for hanging them from a crane over the fire graced a few of the better-equipped and wealthier early American hearths, the all-purpose cooking kettle was again the implement most often used for this procedure. In poaching, food is gently cooked in a barely simmering liquid such as water, wine, or *court bouillon* on a flat strainer or pierced tray which permits easy removal and draining of the food when it is done.

To poach eggs in the cook's kettle, one can use the individual metal egg-poachers found in hardware stores. If you don't have these, vigorously stir the hot poaching water until it swirls around the sides of the pot. Then gently ease in a raw egg by slipping it out of its shell into the swirling water's vortex. The circular action of the hot water will "poach" the egg while preserving its round shape.

To poach larger foods, such as a fish, place a small circular rack outfitted with two large hooks at either edge (hooks can be improvised from coat-hanger wire) in the bottom of the kettle. These hooks will serve as handles for lifting out the fish and draining off the cooking liquid. Place the fish on your rack and cover the pot, poaching until done. And don't despair if your fish is larger than the diameter of your cooking pot. This is a common problem and can be remedied by tucking the fish's tail in its mouth so that it conforms to the circular shape of the kettle, a trick early American cooks frequently relied upon.

To perform many of the above cooking tasks with a small amount of food, the contemporary chef, as did her early American counterpart, will find the posnet a useful alternative to the large cook's kettle. If you are fortunate enough to own an antique example of this cooking implement or even a reproduction, how it is used in a fireplace will be obvious in its design. The posnet sits on the hearth over a small pile of hot coals, raked or shoveled forward from your central cooking fire. Its short legs and regular pot handle are perfectly designed for this application. Proceed with your cooking, refreshing the coals underneath the pot as needed to maintain a steady cooking temperature. Adding more coals will raise the cooking temperature, removing coals will lower it. If you don't happen to have a posnet in your inventory, any ordinary kitchen saucepan, placed on a trivet to raise it above the coals, is a simple and satisfactory substitute.

The Teakettle

Before we finish this chapter, we feel we can't omit at least a passing mention of another boiling device, the teakettle. Nothing is more pleasing on a brisk winter's day than a hot cup of tea, and a teakettle also is a hospitable sight in your fireplace.

Eighteenth-century Americans doted on their afternoon tea, in part because of the customs of their English ancestry and also because of their poorly

A special teakettle with a "tilter" (pictured) is a rare commodity, but simplifies pouring tea from a heavy, hot pot over the fire. A "tilter" pot hook which a blacksmith can easily make for you will adapt any ordinary kettle to fireplace use and will also permit the cook to tip her kettle without removing it.

heated homes. And until the infamous tax on tea made it unpopular and unpatriotic, afternoon tea was a widespread ritual and a time for the ladies to socialize, gossip, and take a breather from the day's activities—the original coffee break. Elaborate china tea sets and silver tea balls and strainers, many of which now exist solely in museums, were some of the attendant accessories used to prepare and serve tea in early America, where they were among the most highly prized possessions owned by a housewife.

Early teakettles for heating water for tea, and for other cooking purposes in the fireplace, were usually cast of iron and were oversized affairs when compared with today's models. They were very heavy and generally were hung from the crane on an S hook. Some of these early teakettles had three small feet, which allowed the cook to sit the kettle on the hearth. Occasionally these iron kettles displayed innovative tilters, devices which permitted the cook to pour water from the heavy, hot kettle without requiring her to lift it off the crane. Tilters consisted of long, stationary lever-like handles attached to the kettle body between its spout and lid. To pour hot water from the kettle, the cook simply pushed down on the tilter, which tipped the kettle's spout downward, emptying its contents into a waiting cup.

Also developed for use with the teakettle were separate tilters. These were really modified pothooks which hung from the crane. They worked on the same leverage principle as the attached tilters, but their advantage was that they transformed any ordinary teakettle into one from which the cook could pour hot water without removing it from the crane.

In wealthier homes, probably the heavy duty iron teakettles were relegated to use in the kitchen fireplaces. In these households, most likely, the lighter-weight kettles made of the more expensive and attractive metals, such as copper and brass, were brought to the dining room and tea tables. These fancier teakettles are often pictured warming before the fire on fancy, tall trivets called footmen.

Old teakettles are rare and sought-after antiques. The most scarce and expensive are those with attached tilters, but even the separate tilter-pothook accessories are very rare. Still one can readily have a reproduction tilter or a double-pronged pothook (to give it more stability) fabricated to suspend your twentieth-century kitchen teakettle over the fire. And if you don't have a crane in your fireplace, a trivet will complete a modern pot's transition from cooktop to hearth.

———➤ **6** ◄———

Frying and Sautéing

In Early
America

hile Southern cooks were famous for their ability to prepare an entire—and delicious—meal in a frying pan, fried foods did not enjoy this same degree of popularity with fireplace cooks throughout America. Deep-fat frying over live coals, near an open fire, was inherently too dangerous. Wooden cooking utensils, spoons, and spatulas threatened to catch fire when they came in contact with the nearly boiling hot oil. And the hot fat could easily spatter, or the frying pan could tip, spilling its contents, and seriously burning the cook or an unwary child. Such accidents could also cause disastrous fires. A fire each week was recorded during the first winter in Boston, and at Plimoth Plantation, one winter, seven of its thirty-two buildings burned to the ground. Frying food was also in need of constant surveillance to ensure that it cooked properly. The earliest fireplace cooks were not willing or able to lavish such serious attention on their cooking activities, since complicated meal preparation usually meant that some other pressing chore would be shortchanged or ignored. Fried food was also not stylish. Mrs. Bradley described frying as " . . . a coarse and greasy Kind of Cookery, in Fashion in the Country, where there are great Appetites, and strong Stomachs, but is at present entirely left off in genteel Families. . . ."

Despite these drawbacks, a number of delicious foods were prepared by frying them at the hearth. Among these delicacies the most famous recipe was for chicken dredged in flour or dipped in batter and then fried in oil—our now popular Southern fried chicken. It was introduced by the well-known Southern cook, Mrs. Randolph. Other foods frequently fried were small fish and oysters. But beef and other meats were usually thinly sliced into steaks and sautéed rather than deep-fat fried.

Toasts for garnishing dishes, fritters and doughnuts of infinite variety, and hush puppies were also commonly cooked in hot fat by fireplace chefs. Hush

81

puppies were a cornmeal-based batter bread that were cooked by dropping spoonfuls of the mixture into hot fat. It was a favorite dish of hunters, since it was easily prepared at their campfires, and it is from them that this food derived its name. As the hush puppies cooked, their tantalizing aroma made the hunters' hungry dogs howl in eager anticipation of dinner. To quiet them, the hunter often tossed a piece of the bread to his hounds, admonishing them, "Hush, puppies."

Eggs were also fried by fireplace cooks. In addition to the more usual preparation of sautéing scrambled eggs, omelets, or "sunnyside up" eggs, in a small amount of butter, early cooks also fried raw eggs into a round ball by breaking them into the vortex of very hot swirling fat. These deep-fried eggs were generally used as a garnish for other dishes, rather than as a breakfast or supper entrée.

Less frequently fried or sautéed by early American cooks were vegetables. But some avant garde cookbooks of the day departed from the norm and recommended, instead of the usual boiling, sautéing of sliced potatoes. These potatoes were the first home fries consumed at the American table. Eggplant was another vegetable that fireplace cooks were encouraged to fry. An early recipe for fried eggplant directed that it be cut into strips and breaded before it was immersed in the hot fat.

For deep-fat frying and sautéing, the fireplace cook had a number of implements at her disposal. Among them was a large, long-handled frying pan.

Large, long-handled frying pans were often used in early American kitchens. Their exceptional handles kept the cook at a comfortable distance from the fire's heat and her long skirts safely away from its flame. These pans were usually placed on special trivets with a bracket which held their handle up. Coals were placed under the pan to cook the food.

And its handle was long—often extending to as much as three feet or more. These handles permitted the cook to fry her food while she remained standing, and kept her long skirts at a safe distance from the treacherous hot fat in the pan. These frying pans were placed on trivets with generous amounts of coals under them to provide the heat necessary for these cooking activities. Sometimes the supporting trivets had a sliding bracket, or rest, to balance the extraordinary long handles of these pans. The rest could support the handle independently, thereby freeing the cook to move closer to inspect or turn her frying food, or to attend to other tasks nearby. But even with this special aid, a frying pan on a trivet was a precarious arrangement at best, and one that was liable to tip over at the slightest provocation.

A more stable design for frying vessels was incorporated in the frying pans that stood over the coals on their own three legs. These pans were affectionately called "spiders" by the early American housewife. Their spindly legs, emanating from the blackened round frying pan, made them resemble overgrown spiders. Spiders came in various sizes and heights, and were much safer

Doughnut kettle for frying doughnuts and fritters is suspended from the crane on a two pronged pothook to give it extra stability.

for fireplace frying than the large frying pans. In addition to the extra stability afforded by their attached legs, their heavier weight (they were usually cast of iron) made them less likely to be knocked over accidentally than lighter implements were.

Two other implements widely used for frying and sautéing by the fireplace cook were the doughnut kettle and the hanging griddle. Doughnut kettles were shallow, cast iron pots with a bail by which the cook hung them from her crane. A double-pronged pothook was probably used for hanging these pots, since a single S hook would have not provided enough stability for this wide, shallow pan to permit safe frying. The hanging griddle, discussed earlier in Chapter 3, Baking, was also used for frying in a small amount of oil, the technique we know as sautéing. Potatoes, scrambled eggs, and French toast were just a few of the foods that could be "fried" or sautéed on this implement.

The common medium for frying foods used by the early American cook was either hog's lard or beef drippings. Butter and olive oil (also known as sweet oil) were just too expensive, though for sautéing, which used a smaller quantity of fat, butter was sometimes used, as it improved the flavor of the final product. When frying, Mrs. Bradley mentioned that the pan should be clean and the fire brisk. "... Smoak will get in if there be any." Other early cookbook authors also recommended that the frying oil be brought to the boiling point before the food was put into it. The food should fry quickly, they specified, but not allowed to become too dark. Eliza Leslie advised frying small fish, such as flounder and perch, five minutes on each side, in hot lard that covered them completely. She also suggested a unique way of testing the temperature of the oil for frying. "You may know when the lard or dripping is hot enough, by dipping in the tail of one of the fish. If it becomes crisp immediately, the lard is in a proper state for frying." When the food was cooked to the desired degree of doneness, it was removed from the hot oil with a regular spatula or a modified version with drainage holes, called a fish slice, and placed on a coarse towel to absorb the excess fat before serving.

Techniques for Today

Although today's modern kitchens have vastly improved the safety of frying, and perhaps made it a more popular method of food preparation than it was, it still remains as dangerous a technique to perform in one's fireplace today as it was 150 years ago. For this reason, we can't honestly recommend deep-fat frying at the open hearth to our readers. It's just too risky. But since any general discussion of food preparation and cooking techniques would be incomplete without mentioning it, and its safer sister, sautéing, we have included our observations on how to most safely and easily execute these two techniques in your fireplace.

Deep-Fat Frying: The Spider and the Dutch Oven

If you must deep-fat fry in your fireplace, the safest two implements at your disposal are an antique spider and your Dutch oven. Both implements are most stable on the hearth floor. And in fact, some books on cooking with cast iron implements even recommend that the first time you cook in a new Dutch oven you fry in it, as this is an easy and reliable way of seasoning its new surfaces. Both spider and Dutch oven will permit deep-fat frying, but of the two we slightly prefer the Dutch oven. The average Dutch oven will, in general, hold more oil than most spiders. Its straight, deep sides can in some instances accommodate a frying basket. It comes already equipped with a lid, which you may need to ensure thorough cooking of thicker pieces of food, such as chicken. And reproduction Dutch ovens are readily available, while antique spiders are fairly uncommon, and new ones are not being mass-produced, to our knowledge.

To fry your food in either of these implements, place them over a healthy bed of coals and add enough vegetable oil or shortening to reach the level necessary for frying your food. Do not fill the pan to its edge, but leave enough room for the displacement caused by the addition of the food to be fried, and for the bubbling and rolling motion caused by the oil as it cooks the food. Let the oil preheat over the coals and test its readiness for frying with a piece of bread. Frying oil should be hot enough so that a cube of dry bread, dropped into it, becomes golden brown in about a minute's time. Delicate wisps of smoke will rise from the surface of the oil at this temperature. If the whole surface of the pot is smoking, the oil is too hot.

To begin frying, gently ease your batter-dipped or floured food into the hot fat one or two pieces at a time with a metal spatula or tongs. Do not crowd them, or add too many at once, as this will lower the temperature of the oil and your food will not turn out as crisp and light as it should. Remove the pieces as they are cooked and drain on paper toweling placed on the shelf of a reflector bake oven or on a cookie sheet. Place cooked food near the fire to keep it warm while you fry the remaining food. When you are frying thicker foods, such as chicken parts, it also may be necessary to place a lid on the frying pot to ensure the food is thoroughly cooked when the outside crust appears browned.

Fresh coals may have to be shoveled under the spider or Dutch oven in order to maintain an adequate temperature for frying successive batches of food. To do this, carefully push the fresh embers under the spider or the Dutch oven with a fireplace shovel. Do this with extreme caution so as not to get any embers into the hot oil, or to knock over the frying vessel. Never, under any circumstances, should you lift the spider or Dutch oven when it is filled with hot oil—this despite the fact that lifting the cooking pot is the standard, and generally easiest, method of replenishing coals under the Dutch oven, and is advised in the baking chapter and elsewhere in this book. Nor should you ever consider deep-fat frying in a pot suspended from the crane, such as in an antique doughnut kettle you may own, as the potential for the hot fat to tip over on the cook or into the fire is too great.

Sautéing: The Spider and the Hanging Griddle

Now that we have thoroughly discouraged you from deep-fat frying in your fireplace, we would like to discuss the ease and merits of an alternative method of frying at your hearth, sautéing. Many implements lend themselves readily to sautéing, the cooking of food in a small amount of fat. Among these, especially useful for fireplace sautéing is the spider, the long-handled antique frying pan (or even a modern short-handled one for that matter) placed on a trivet, and the hanging griddle.

Sautéing on, or in, any of these three implements is a simple process, much the same from one utensil to another. First, a small amount of oil or butter, or a combination of the two, should be applied to their slightly preheated surfaces. Mixing the oil with the butter will increase the temperature to which the butter can be heated before it burns—a useful trick if it takes a long time to cook your food. Place the food to be sautéed in the hot fat and let it cook until done on one side. Turn food with a metal spatula or tongs and continue cooking on the other side. Remove the food and serve. Or, if you wish, keep it warm while you prepare a sauce to serve with it. To do this, deglaze the sautéing pan by adding a small amount of wine or other liquid, such as chicken broth, to the fats and juices left in it. Cook slightly, stirring with a wisk until sauce is slightly reduced in quantity and thickened. (This last step will not be possible on the griddle.)

To provide the heat necessary for sautéing, frying pans and spiders rely on a supply of hot coals placed under their frying surfaces. And even the hanging griddle, which is usually hung on the crane by the cook, could be used for

Sautéing in a small spider.

sautéing on the hearth floor too, if it is a footed model, with legs tall enough to permit placing a layer of coals under it. A footless hanging griddle can be placed on a trivet to adapt it to hearth sautéing, too. And in sautéing, unlike deep-fat frying, these pans can usually be lifted safely if it becomes necessary to replenish their cooking coals.

Sautéing can also be done on a hanging griddle, provided only a small amount of fat is needed. Here French toast is being browned in butter.

7

Planning a Feast
from Your Fireplace

Social Advantages of Fireplace Cooking

In addition to its novelty, the pure fun of it, and the wonderful flavor it imparts to food, fireplace cooking and entertaining can be very compatible dinner partners. This is especially true if your fireplace is located in a family or living room, the usual home entertaining area. Cooking in the living room, as strange as it may sound, affords some real advantages for the cook and host or hostess. It resolves a common dilemma with which he or she is often faced: the choice of either laboring alone over final meal details in a separate kitchen, leaving guests to fend for themselves or with a spouse to entertain them; or having company wander into a hot, messy, and cramped dinner-party kitchen for a peek in the oven and a chat with the cook.

Picture instead: the soup gently simmering in the gypsy kettle, a bread or pie baking in the Dutch oven, and a roast browning before the fire on a spit. All supervised out of the corner of the chef's watchful eye, while the chef sits and enjoys a drink with the company. And, if an especially ambitious array of fireplace foods is planned, a guest is always near at hand, and more than willing, we have found, to turn the spit or baste the meat.

When dinner is completed, it can be served with great style directly from many of the unique open-hearth cooking pots and implements, cutting down on the use of serving platters to wash up later. For example, soup and other one-pot meals can be ladled directly from the interesting kettle in which they were cooked into individual bowls. A planked fish can be most strikingly presented, garnished, and brought to the table right on the rustic board on which it was roasted.

Second helpings, as well as dinner plates, are easily kept warm and at arm's reach at the fire's edge, eliminating the need for electric hot trays or a dash to the kitchen oven.

The energy savings possible with fireplace cooking also make it attractive for entertaining. Since many of us light a fire to make a room more inviting for guests, why not be thrifty as well, and use this heat to cook dinner for them, too?

And, a final word on its merits for entertaining: fireplace cooking is an intriguing performance for old friends and provides a great topic of conversation for new ones.

Menus and Tips for Entertaining

Practice fireplace cooking techniques and recipes on family before inviting company. The more complicated techniques or recipes may require a few trial runs before you feel completely comfortable with their execution and are satisfied with the results. While cooking in a fireplace is easy once you get the knack of it, the new skills and different tempo involved may seem awkward and even intimidating, at first, for the beginner.

Build up to five-course fireplace dinners slowly. Start with simple menus first, in which only one food is cooked in the fireplace and the rest are prepared ahead of time, preferably the night before, in your modern kitchen.

Set up your hearth cooking area before your guests arrive with all the equipment you're likely to need, to avoid countless trips to your regular kitchen for pot-holders, paper towels, serving platters, or carving knives.

Allow plenty of time for the food to cook. Open-hearth cooking times are not precise, but, since in general it takes slightly longer to cook food in your fireplace than with a modern appliance, we always have plenty of hors d'oeuvres on hand or serve a soup course to help hungry guests (and the cook) pass the time more patiently in case of a delay.

Keep in mind that no matter how proficient a fireplace chef you become, cooking for a large crowd on the open hearth may not be practical. Cooking food in large quantities in the fireplace can lose its novelty, and may become only hot, time-consuming, and a great deal of work. Even in our huge pre-Revolutionary walk-in hearth, we usually limit our fireplace dinners to eight, since most of the standard hearth cooking pots and implements have the capacity to cook only enough food to serve this number at one time.

On special occasions, when a large crowd is to be fed, we get around this problem by preparing a chili, or other substantial one-pot meal, in a gypsy kettle, a pot that is more readily found in the larger sizes, and accompany it with lots of extras fixed beforehand in our regular kitchens. And for a very festive occasion, if your fireplace is big enough, a professional restaurant spit can be rented to roast a suckling pig before the fire.

Finally, even though you're the hostess, don't lose sight of the fact that you're the chef, as well. Tending a fire and cooking with it can be a dirty, hot, and sometimes hazardous activity, especially in a fashionable hostess gown. So dress sensibly—Chapter 2, The Cooking Fire, discusses the appropriate apparel for fireplace cooking.

Menus for Fireplace Repasts

Following are menus, both simple and elaborate, suitable for entertaining family and friends at the hearth. The starred recipes can be found in the next chapter, Recipes for a Feast From Your Fireplace, with directions for cooking them in your fireplace. Many of the other foods in the menus for which we have not supplied recipes can be prepared in your fireplace, as well. For these, we have indicated the implement of choice to use in their preparation. Still other foods included in these menus can be prepared ahead of time, even the night before, to supplement a special or complicated fireplace dish or to simplify the fireplace cooking part of the meal for a fledgling hearth-side cook. Also, don't ignore the potential of ready-made foods available in the freezer compartment of your supermarket. These can be heated and served right from your fireplace as easily as they can from your modern kitchen, and can round out a fireplace broiled steak entrée for a working homemaker.

Down on the Farm Breakfast

Bacon (fried on the hanging griddle).

Eggs (scrambled in the spider).

Cornmeal biscuits* or toast (branded by a decorative hearth toaster) with freshly churned butter and homemade jam.

Late Risers' Breakfasts

Fruit juice.

Apple scrapple* *or* bannocks* and Canadian bacon (sautéed in the spider).

Continental Breakfast

Freshly squeezed orange juice.

French toast* with powdered sugar or Vermont maple syrup.

Sunday Brunch

Bloody Marys.

Bruncheon eggs* on English muffins*.

Fresh fruit salad.

Apple coffee cake*.

Fisherman's Luck Lunch

Manhattan clam chowder*.

Perfect corn bread*.

Blueberry cake*.

Skating Party Lunch

> Hearty meatball soup*.
>
> Oatmeal bread*.
>
> Ember glazed baked apples*.
>
> Brownies*.

After The Game

> Pea soup (gypsy kettle).
>
> Sautéed pork roll on toasted bagels (spider or griddle and toaster).
>
> Jersey lightning fritters*.

Indian Birthday Luncheon

> Bear burgers (hamburgers prepared on the gridiron).
>
> Roots, nuts, and berries (carrot sticks, peanuts, and raisins).
>
> S'mores*.

Help Yourself "Rose Bowl" Lunch

> Lentils and kielbasa*.
>
> Anadama bread*.
>
> Poached spiced pears* and cookies.

French Market Lunch

> Fresh mussel stew* or quiche*.
>
> Bibb lettuce salad.
>
> French bread and cheese.
>
> Chocolate Mousse.

Midday Sunday Dinner

> Consommé with mushroom slices (gypsy kettle).
>
> Cornish hens with tarragon butter*.
>
> Rice pilaf.
>
> Broccoli with lemon butter (gypsy kettle or spider).
>
> Sautéed bananas*.

All American Dinner

> Pumpkin peanut soup*.
>
> Prime Ribs of Beef.
>
> Yorkshire pudding (baked in Dutch oven).
>
> Snap beans savory butter (gypsy kettle or spider).
>
> Apple pie*.

Company's Coming

    Stuffed mushrooms (baked in Dutch oven).

    Filet mignon steaks*.

    Baked potatoes (wrapped in foil and cooked in embers).

    Bibb lettuce salad.

    Cream puffs filled with ice cream and topped with chocolate sauce (warmed at hearth).

Traditional Thanksgiving Dinner

    Oyster stew (gypsy kettle).

    Roast capon or turkey (on spit or in tin kitchen).

    Cranberry sauce.

    Brussels sprouts and glazed chestnuts (gypsy kettle or spider).

    String beans (gypsy kettle).

    Sweet potato buns*.

    Pumpkin pudding* or pumpkin pie.

Christmas Dinner Spectacular

    Relish tray: radishes, celery, olives.

    Cream of onion soup (gypsy kettle).

    Roast suckling pig* with stuffing.

    Yam pie*.

    Buttered peas and mint (spider).

    Holiday plum pudding* with hard sauce.

Chinese Dinner

    Dim sum.

    Egg drop soup*.

    Chinese duck*.

    Rice (Dutch oven).

    Spicy cucumber salad.

    Fresh melon and fortune cookies.

Ides of March Dinner

    Planked shad fillets*.

    Fresh asparagus (gypsy kettle).

    Scalloped potatoes*.

    Mixed Salad.

    Pecan pie* with whipped cream.

Spring Company Dinner

    Artichokes with hollandaise (gypsy kettle and saucepan).

    Lamb chops (gridiron).

    Herb stuffed tomatoes*.

    Baked potatoes with sour cream and chives (bake in foil in embers).

    Crème caramel* and springerle cookies*.

One-Dish Family Supper

    Fruited pork pie* or chicken pie*.

    Garden salad.

    Whole wheat bread.

    Gingerbread*.

New England Saturday Night Supper

    Yankee baked beans*.

    Steamed Boston brown bread*.

    Cole slaw.

    Fresh fruit with cookies.

South-of-the-Border Supper

    Assorted crackers and cheeses.

    Raw vegetables and dip.

    Chili*.

    Jalapeno corn bread*.

Festive Friday Night Fish

    Hot grapefruit halves*.

    Stuffed sea bass*.

    Parsley potatoes (spider).

    Sautéed cherry tomatoes (spider).

    Apricot and apple steamed pudding*.

Vegetarian Special

    Zucchini frittata*.

    Mushroom and sprout salad.

    Pita bread.

    Carrot cake*.

Italian Dinner

Antipasto salad.

Gnocchi*.

Lasagna (Dutch oven).

Fragrant herb bread*.

Melon balls with anisette.

New Year's Eve Supper

Hot cranberry punch*.

Raclette*.

Boiled potatoes (gypsy kettle).

Pickled vegetables (onions and gherkin pickles are traditional).

Angel cake with ice cream and topped with hot fudge sauce (heat sauce at hearth).

Dessert Party

Wafers*, waffles*, or Jersey lightning fritters*.

Coffee and tea brewed at the hearth.

Cocktail Party

Mulled cider*.

Assorted Hors d'Oeuvres: fireplace tempura*. Swedish meatballs, spare ribs, etc. fixed in the fireplace, plus an assortment made ahead of time such as: shrimp remoulade, melon with prosciutto, crackers and cheese.

8

Recipes for a Feast from Your Fireplace with Special Directions for Cooking Them at Your Hearth

ow that we have outlined in theory how to execute all the basic cooking techniques in a fireplace and plan a party at your hearth, here are some recipes you can use to put these new skills into practice. We have cooked and enjoyed many foods in our fireplaces, and the following collection of sixty recipes represents a sampling of these, chosen to illustrate the use of every implement and cooking technique discussed in this book. All the fireplace implements and cooking techniques discussed in preceding chapters are utilized at least once, and some, because of their reliability, ease of use, and versatility (notably the Dutch oven), are mentioned more frequently.

These recipes were written expressly for open-hearth cooking, and some of the directions are noticeably unlike anything encountered in any other contemporary cookbook. So here are a few guidelines on how to interpret and use them.

Before you begin mixing up ingredients for a dish, we recommend that you read the recipe all the way through. It may be necessary to refresh your memory by referring to earlier accounts of the procedure for using an implement or executing a fireplace cooking technique required by the recipe, since in the interest of saving space and avoiding repetition, we have not repeated in each recipe every last step and fine point of each implement's use, or the details of executing specific fireplace techniques. To review this information in its entirety, refer back to the Techniques for Today sections of the appropriate chapters.

The recipes are arranged as follows: The ingredients are listed first, in the order in which they are used, with substitutions noted. Unless otherwise specified, eggs are large, and flour all-purpose. Next comes the preparation of the ingredients—cutting, dicing, sifting, peeling, etc.—and their method of mixing and cooking. After this comes the food's test for doneness and the approximate number of people the recipe serves. Following the recipe and its general method, are remarks on the fireplace equipment, heat, and cooking time, and, finally, tips on successfully and easily preparing and serving each particular food at the hearth.

Under hearth equipment, the implement or pot of choice is listed first. If you don't happen to have this item in your inventory, other pots or improvised equivalents are listed next. These will allow you to cook the food in your fireplace with the same results as you would achieve with the implement itself. In some cases no satisfactory alternative utensil exists. In these cases, you may have to wait to try the recipe.

Under heat, general cooking temperatures or ranges are given. For more information on using and controlling the heat of the fire with the implement or technique specified, again refer back to the Techniques for Today sections in the appropriate chapters to find a detailed description of the regulation of the fire's heat for that procedure.

Approximate cooking times are also given. While these are fairly accurate, be sure to test the food for doneness before serving. Meat thermometers and cake testers are essential for thicker cakes and roasts.

And finally, Fireplace Tips are a catch-all for remarks on some of the special aspects of cooking and serving a particular food at the hearth.

A few of the more complicated recipes direct you to mix or do preliminary cooking of ingredients in your kitchen, and to do only the final cooking of the food at the fireplace. This is for the chef's convenience in certain recipes; but it is a suggestion that may well be utilized in many other recipes, too, since most fireplaces used for cooking today are not in or near your kitchen where all your spices, mixing bowls, baking pans, etc., are stored and handy.

Here, then, are the recipes. A quick glance will reveal that they reflect the ethnic variety and varied tastes of Americans today. This was intentional, so as not to limit your fireplace cooking horizons solely to early American dishes, which were primarily English fare. We don't want you to feel it is in any way sacrilegious to roast a duck, Chinese style, in your tin kitchen, or bake an Italian pizza in your Dutch oven.

For the purist, an abundance of excellent cookbooks covering American recipes and menus can be found on the shelves of most public libraries. A number of these books were especially helpful to us in our research, and we have identified them for your convenience in the bibliography at the back of this book. Remember, when adapting recipes from any other source for fireplace cooking, that it may take slightly longer to cook food in your fireplace than it does with a modern appliance.

Beverages, Appetizers, and Soups

Mulled Cider

Stud an orange or an apple with 6 cloves. Fill gypsy kettle 3/4 full with apple cider. Add clove-studded fruit and simmer. The aroma that arises will fill your home with good cheer.

This recipe can be changed to suit your whim or larder. A lemon can be used instead of the orange or apple or combined with them. A cinnamon stick, grated nutmeg, or a dash of applejack can be added to each cup as it is served.

Hot Cranberry Punch

4 cups cranberry juice	1 cinnamon stick
4 cups apple juice	4 whole cloves
1 cup pear juice	1 lemon, thinly sliced
	2 apples, cored and cut in wedges*

Combine cranberry, apple, and pear juices in gypsy kettle. Add spices and lemon slices. Bring to boiling point, lower heat, and simmer 5 minutes. Ladle into mugs and serve with wedge of apple.

Serves: 8.

Hearth Equipment: gypsy kettle.

Heat: hot to bring to a boil, and then lower 5 minutes to a simmer.

*Dip apple wedges in lemon juice to keep them from discoloring.

Hot Grapefruit Halves

3 large grapefruits   6 tbsp. honey*

Cut grapefruits in half, loosen sections from membrane, and skin with a small serrated grapefruit knife. Top each half with 1 tbsp. of honey.

Place grapefruit on hanging griddle to heat. When warm, glaze tops by holding a red hot coal (with tongs) over honey coating for a few moments.
Serves: 6.
Hearth Equipment: hanging griddle, reflector bake oven, or pan on a trivet, ember tongs or metal kitchen or barbecue tongs.
Heat: moderate.
Approximate Cooking Time: 10–15 minutes.
Fireplace Tip: Grapefruit halves can also be wrapped in foil and baked Indian-style in the hot embers. After heated through, open foil and proceed to brown off tops as directed above.

* *Use brown sugar if you prefer.*

Gnocchi Hors d'oeuvres

1/2 cup butter   4 cups milk
1/2 cup farina   2 eggs
1/2 cup cornstarch   1 cup grated parmesan cheese
1/4 tsp. salt   4 tbsp. butter

In your kitchen: Melt butter in top of double boiler. Combine farina, cornstarch, and salt; stir into butter. Heat milk and add, cooking over direct heat, and stirring vigorously until very thick. Replace pan over boiling water, cover and cook 10 minutes longer. Lightly beat eggs and stir into farina mixture with cheese. Spread 3/4-inch thick in a well-buttered 8-x-8-inch pan, and chill until firm in refrigerator. (Will keep 4 days.)

At the fireplace: Cut Gnocchi into 1-inch rounds, squares, or diamonds (trimmings can be pressed together and recut). Melt 4 tbsp. butter in spider or posnet and dip each shape in it. Preheat hanging griddle and grease. Sauté Gnocchi, turning once with spatula.
Yield: 36 hors d'oeuvres.
Hearth Equipment: spider, posnet, or small saucepan on a trivet, hanging griddle or large frying pan on a trivet.
Heat: low for melting butter; moderate for sautéing Gnocchi.
Approximate Sautéing Time: 5 minutes each side.

Fireplace Tempura

1 can beer
1 1/2 cups flour
3-4 cups raw vegetables and/or
    fish: Zucchini chips, carrot
    sticks, onion rings, whole
    mushrooms, broccoli, sprigs
    of parsley, shrimp, or fillets
    of any firm-fleshed fish cut
    into small thick slices.

Dipping Sauce

1/2 cup soy sauce
1/2 cup sherry or white wine
1/8 tsp. ground ginger (or 1/2
    tsp. freshly grated)

cooking oil to fill spider to a
    depth of 1 1/2 inches

Whisk together beer and flour until smooth. Let sit at room temperature for 1 hour or more. Prepare vegetables and/or fish, and refrigerate.

Heat oil to hot. Test temperature by dropping a bit of batter or a fresh bread cube into it. They should brown quickly. Dip vegetables and fish into batter, letting excess drip back into bowl, and gently place a few at a time in hot oil. Fry, turning as necessary with a fork, until puffed and golden brown on all sides. Remove and drain on paper towels. Continue until all morsels are cooked. Serve with dipping sauce.

Serves: 6-8.

Hearth Equipment: spider, or bottom of Dutch oven.

Heat: high. Don't put too many pieces of batter-coated food into the pan at one time, as they will lower the temperature of the oil below its frying point.

Approximate Frying Time: 5 minutes.

Fireplace Tip: Be extremely careful when frying over coals. Don't let any embers get into the oil or allow it to splatter. Batches of tempura can be served immediately or kept warm near the fire in a reflector bake oven or on a piece of aluminum foil. We find we can never make enough of these delicious morsels, or make them fast enough!

Manhattan Clam Chowder

6 slices bacon
2 onions
2 carrots
3 ribs of celery with tops
1 green pepper
2 large potatoes
1 (28 oz.) can tomatoes

1 bay leaf
1 tsp. thyme
2 cups beef bouillon
4 cups clams with liquor*
1/4 cup parsley
salt and freshly ground
    black pepper

Chop bacon and sauté in gypsy kettle. Dice onions, carrots, celery and green pepper, and add, cooking until soft but not brown. Peel and cube potatoes and add with tomatoes, seasonings, and beef bouillon. Bring to a boil and simmer 1 hour. Chop clams, and add with liquor and parsley, chopped, to chowder. Simmer 3 minutes longer.** Season with salt and freshly ground black pepper to taste, and serve.

Serves: 6.

Hearth Equipment: gypsy kettle.

Heat: High to boil; moderate to low to simmer chowder.

Approximate Cooking Time: 1 hour 10 minutes.

* *Use fresh, frozen, or canned clams.*
** *Do not allow chowder to boil after clams have been added, as they will toughen.*

Hearty Meatball Soup

3 carrots	1 (8 oz.) can tomatoes
2 parsnips	1/4 tsp. rosemary
2 stalks celery	1/4 cup raw rice
2 medium onions	1/2 lb. ground beef*
1 1/2 qts. beef stock	salt and freshly ground
	black pepper

Dice carrots, parsnips, celery, and onions; break up tomatoes in liquid. Combine all ingredients, except for meat and salt and pepper, in a gypsy kettle and bring to a boil. Lower temperature and simmer soup gently for 1 hour. Meanwhile shape meat into small balls and brown in butter or oil in a spider. Add to soup after it has cooked for 1 hour; simmer 10 minutes longer, stirring occasionally. Season with salt and freshly ground black pepper to taste, and serve.

Serves: 4.

Hearth Equipment: gypsy kettle, and spider, or pan frying on a trivet.

Heat: High to boil and lower to simmer soup, moderate to sauté meatballs.

Approximate Cooking Time: 1 1/2 hours.

Fireplace Tip: Soups improve with the length of cooking time. Just add more beef stock if it gets too thick for your taste.

* *Ground lamb could be substituted for the beef.*

Pumpkin Peanut Soup

1 medium onion	3 cups chicken broth
2 ribs of celery with tops	1/4 cup peanut butter
3 tbsp. butter	1/4 tsp. summer savory*
2 sprigs parsley	salt and freshly ground pepper to taste
2 cups canned pumpkin	1/2 cup light cream

Chop onion and celery, and lightly sauté in butter in gypsy kettle. Chop parsley and add to kettle with remaining ingredients, except for salt, pepper, and cream. Simmer 15 minutes. Season with salt and pepper to taste, and, just before serving, add cream. If soup is to be held for a time at the hearth, do not add the light cream. Instead, serve a steaming cup of soup topped with a dollop of whipped, heavy cream.

Serves: 4.

Hearth Equipment: gypsy kettle.

Heat: moderate to low for sautéing; low for simmering.

Approximate Cooking Time: 25 minutes.

* *Thyme could be substituted for savory.*

Egg Drop Soup

1 qt. rich chicken broth	salt and white pepper to taste
1 egg	1 scallion

Heat broth in gypsy kettle to boiling point; lower temperature to simmering. Lightly beat egg and dribble very slowly into hot soup, stirring all the while with a chopstick or long-handled fork so swirling soup cooks egg in long strings or "drops." Taste soup and season if needed with salt and a bit of white pepper. Serve garnished with trimmed, minced scallions, green end included for color.

Serves: 4.

Hearth Equipment: gypsy kettle.

Heat: high, then low.

Approximate Cooking Time: 15 minutes.

Entrées and Accompaniments

Apple Scrapple

1/2 lb. bulk sausage	1/2 cup cold water
1/2 cup yellow cornmeal	1/2 cup boiling water
1/2 tsp. salt	1 cup applesauce
butter	flour

In your kitchen: Crumble sausage and cook in skillet until it is well done. Drain off fat. In a saucepan combine cornmeal and salt, gradually stir in cold water, then add boiling water. Cook over low heat, stirring constantly until thickened. Cover and continue cooking over low heat for 10 minutes. Fold in drained sausage and applesauce. Turn scrapple mixture into a small loaf pan. Cover and chill in refrigerator until firm—several hours or overnight.

At the fireplace: Loosen scrapple from sides of pan with a sharp knife and turn out on board. Cut into slices, dip each in flour. Preheat spider and melt butter in it. Sauté scrapple slices until browned on both sides, turning once.

Serves: 4–6.
Hearth Equipment: large spider or frying pan on a trivet.
Heat: high.
Approximate Sautéing Time: 3–5 minutes each side.

Bruncheon Eggs

At first glance, this dish involves quite a few steps. A proficient cook could prepare it all by herself, but if helpers are handy, assigning a task to each relieves the pressure and adds to the fun.

Fireplace Sauce	4 slices of Canadian bacon
4 eggs	2 English muffins*

First, prepare the sauce.

Fireplace Sauce

2 tbsp. butter	1/8 tsp. pepper
2 tbsp. flour	1 cup milk
1/4 tsp. salt	1/2 cup mayonnaise

seasonings as desired (one or a combination of the following): 1/4 tsp. curry powder, 1/4 tsp. chili powder, 2 tbsp. chopped pimento, 2 tbsp. parsley, 1 tsp. capers, few drops tabasco sauce, 1 tbsp. chives, 1/2 tsp. dill weed

Melt butter in posnet. Add flour and salt and pepper, cook until bubbly. Gradually add milk. Stir until smooth, and cook until thickened. Stir in mayonnaise and desired seasonings. Keep sauce warm at hearth's edge.

Second, fry bacon and eggs.

Fry bacon and eggs on hanging griddle until done. Keep warm until ready to assemble dish.

Third, toast muffins.

Split muffins by pulling apart with a fork and fingers. Toast in fireplace toaster or in reflector oven.

Finally, assemble bruncheon eggs.

Place 1/2 toasted muffin on plate. Top with slice of bacon, one egg, and a spoonful of sauce.

Serves: 2 very hungry guests or 4 moderately hungry ones.

Hearth Equipment: posnet or saucepan on a trivet; hanging griddle or frying pan on a trivet; fireplace toaster or reflector oven.

Heat: moderate for all techniques.

* *Store-bought muffins are fine for this recipe, but if you are especially ambitious, a recipe for homemade ones is included in the Breads, Muffins and Biscuits section of this chapter.*

Zucchini Frittata

1 tbsp. butter	1/2 tsp. thyme
1 tbsp. oil	salt and freshly ground
1 large onion	black pepper
2 small zucchini	5 eggs
1 tbsp. parsley	

Melt butter and oil in spider. Add coarsely chopped onion and sauté until lightly yellowed. Thinly slice zucchini and add. Continue to sauté until vegetable is cooked, but still crisp. Chop parsley and add to spider, with thyme, and salt and pepper to taste. Beat eggs lightly with a fork and pour over vegetable and seasonings. Allow eggs to set, stir occasionally so uncooked eggs run to bottom of pan. A lid may be used.

Cook until eggs are done. Cut into wedges and serve.*

Serves: This recipe serves 4, but to accommodate the number and appetites to be served, increase or decrease the eggs.

Hearth Equipment: spider or frying pan on a trivet.

Heat: moderate.

Approximate Cooking Time: 7–10 minutes.

* *Any vegetables, fresh or leftover, bits of meat or fish, and cheese may be used in the Frittata. Garlic or any favorite herbs can be substituted or used in addition to the thyme and parsley.*

Cheese Quiche

1 1/2 cups Swiss cheese*	2 cups heavy cream
1 partially baked, 9-inch	1 1/2 tsp. salt
pie shell	dash cayenne pepper
4 eggs	nutmeg, freshly grated

Preheat Dutch oven with rack.

Shred cheese and sprinkle evenly over bottom of pie shell. Lightly beat eggs, combine with cream, salt, and cayenne pepper. Place pie shell with cheese on rack in preheated oven and gently pour in egg and cream mixture. Grate a bit of fresh nutmeg on the surface, and bake until a sharp knife inserted in center comes out clean.

Serves: 4 for lunch; more for appetizers or hors d'oeuvres.

Hearth Equipment: Dutch oven with rack.

Heat: moderate to high. Place slightly more coals underneath oven to set bottom of quiche during the first stages of baking.

Approximate Baking Time: 30 minutes.

* *Gruyère, Jarlsberg or Emmenthaler are especially good. For variation, add bits of precooked bacon, ham, sausage, or vegetables.*

Raclette

Serving Raclette on New Year's Eve is a Swiss tradition supposed to bring good luck. But serving this specialty on any cold winter night is appropriate and delicious.

3 lbs. new potatoes	sweet and dill gherkins
wedge of Raclette cheese*	pickled vegetables
(approx. 3 lbs.)	

Boil potatoes in their jackets in gypsy kettle with skins on. When done, remove from water. Remove the rind from the cheese and place on foil-covered gridiron. Place close to hot coals or fire. Divide potatoes on 6 to 8 plates and keep warm on hearth's edge. As face of cheese melts, scrape it off with a knife and place on one of the plates near the potatoes. Repeat for each serving. Serve with gherkins and pickled vegetables. Watch cheese closely, as it melts very quickly.

Serves: 6 to 8.

Hearth Equipment: gypsy kettle, gridiron or broiling rack supported by two bricks.

Heat: moderate.

Approximate Cooking Time: After the potatoes are boiled, just a few minutes is needed to melt the cheese.

* *Raclette cheese is available in specialty cheese stores. It has a special melting quality. If it is not available, Gruyère or Tilsit may be substituted.*

Fresh Mussel Stew

36 fresh mussels	3/4 cup dry white wine**
3 tbsp. butter	salt and freshly ground
	black pepper
1 clove garlic	1/2 cup cream
3 tbsp. shallots*	3 tbsp. parsley
1 small bay leaf	

Scrub mussels well, de-beard them, and set them aside. In gypsy kettle, heat butter. Mince garlic and shallots and cook slowly in butter until wilted. Add mussels to kettle with wine, bay leaf, and salt and pepper. Cover and simmer gently until mussels open, about 10 minutes. Pour cream over mussels and heat until just warm. Ladle into bowls and sprinkle with chopped parsley.

* *Substitute onion for shallots*
** *Use white vermouth, diluted with water by 1/2, in place of white wine.*

Serves: 4.
Hearth Equipment: gypsy kettle or Dutch oven.
Heat: moderate.
Approximate Cooking Time: 20 minutes.

Lentils and Kielbasa

A hearty stew with a robust aroma.

1 cup lentils	2 lbs. kielbasa
2 onions	1 (1 lb.) can crushed
1 carrot	tomatoes
2 garlic cloves	1 bay leaf
2 tbsp. butter	salt and freshly ground
	black pepper

Rinse lentils and place in gypsy kettle with salted water to cover. Cook, covered, for 20 minutes or until lentils are tender but still hold their shape. Remove lentils from kettle and drain, reserving liquid.

Chop the onions, carrot, and garlic, and sauté in butter in gypsy kettle until slightly browned. Slice sausage and add to pot with tomatoes and seasonings. Simmer together 15 minutes. Add lentils and cook at least 30 minutes more to allow flavors to mingle. Add salt and pepper to taste, and serve.

Serves: 6–8.
Hearth Equipment: gypsy kettle or bottom of Dutch oven.
Heat: moderate.
Approximate Cooking Time: 1 1/2 hours.
Fireplace Tip: This is a dinner that improves with the length of cooking! So let your guests linger, and just add some of the reserved lentil cooking liquid to thin it out if it gets too thick.

Chili

4 strips bacon	1 (1 lb.) can tomatoes
1 medium onion	1 tsp. salt
1 clove garlic	1/2 tsp. freshly ground
	black pepper
1 lb. ground beef	1 15 oz. can kidney beans
1 tbsp. cinnamon	1 12 oz. can corn niblets
1 tbsp. chili powder	

Dice bacon and sauté in gypsy kettle. When crisp, remove pieces with slotted spoon. Dice onion and garlic, add with ground beef, and cook until meat is browned. Remove most of the rendered fat, and add remaining ingredients, except for bacon. Simmer together slowly, adding water if necessary, and season to your tastes. Some like it hot! Add cooked bacon just before serving.

Serves: 4.

Hearth Equipment: gypsy kettle or bottom of Dutch oven.

Heat: moderate to high for frying bacon and sautéing onions, meat, etc.; low for simmering chili.

Approximate Cooking Time: 1 hour.

Fireplace Tip: Chili improves with the length of the cooking time. Just add more water if it gets too thick.

———————◆———————

Chicken Pie

1 (4–5 lb.) chicken	3 tbsp. butter
2 stalks celery	3 tbsp. flour
2 medium carrots	2 tbsp. parsley
1 medium onion	1 cup slivered almonds
2 tsp. salt	1/4 tsp. thyme
1/2 tsp. freshly ground	biscuit or pie dough for
black pepper	top crust
1/2 cup mushrooms	egg wash*

Place chicken in gypsy kettle with coarsely chopped celery, carrots, and onion. Barely cover with water and add salt and pepper. Cover pot and bring to a boil, skim; and simmer until chicken is thoroughly cooked, yet tender. Remove chicken, reserve broth and vegetables. Remove and discard bones and skin from chicken, cut meat into fairly large pieces.

Slice mushrooms and sauté in butter in spider. Sprinkle with flour and combine well. Add 2 cups reserved chicken broth and cook until thickened. Mince parsley, and add, with almonds and thyme, to sauce.

Place chicken and vegetables in casserole, pour in sauce, lifting chicken to allow sauce to seep underneath. Top with biscuit or pie dough with vents to let steam escape. Brush with egg wash for a pretty finish.

Place on a rack in a preheated Dutch oven and bake until the crust is a golden brown and chicken thoroughly heated.

Serves: 4–6.

Hearth Equipment: gypsy kettle, Dutch oven with rack.

Heat: medium high. Place slightly more coals on lid of oven last 10 minutes of baking to brown top crust nicely.

Approximate Baking Time: 40 minutes.

Fireplace Tip: Make sure casserole fits into Dutch oven. Try empty pans in cold oven before beginning recipe.

  * *To make egg wash: Stir together 1 lightly beaten egg with 1 tsp. water.*

Fruited Pork Pie*

1 medium onion, chopped
1 lb. ground pork
1 tsp. oil
4 sweet sausage links, sliced
1 cup cranberries,
    fresh preferred**
1 orange, peeled, seeded,
    and diced
1 small can unsweetened yams

1 cup beef stock or consommé
1/2 bay leaf
1/2 tsp. thyme
salt and freshly ground
    pepper to taste
1/2 cup red wine
unsweetened pie dough
    for top crust
milk to glaze top crust

Preheat Dutch oven.

Sauté together chopped onion and ground pork in oil in a large spider. When cooked, remove, drain, and discard fat. Brown sausage slices. Combine cooked meats and onion with fruits, vegetables, stock, seasonings, and wine in a shallow casserole. Moisten edge of casserole with water. Place pie crust in place and press down on edges to secure, and flute as you would for fruit pie. Slash top to allow steam to escape and brush with milk to glaze.

Place pie on a rack in a preheated Dutch oven and bake until crust is nicely browned.

Serves: 6.

Hearth Equipment: large spider or frying pan on a trivet; Dutch oven with rack.

Heat: sautéing—moderate.

    baking—medium high, slightly more coals on lid last 10 minutes of baking to brown top of pie.

Approximate Baking Time: 1 hour.

Fireplace Tip: Be sure to check depth of casserole in cold Dutch oven before preheating and filling. Allow enough space for both rack and top crust. A pie plate could be used if you don't have a shallow enough casserole.

* *Any favorite stew recipe can be substituted. With a top crust it becomes a meat pie.*
** *A small can of whole cranberry sauce could be substituted.*

Roast Suckling Pig

Unquestionably the *pièce de résistance* of fireplace cooking, and a spectacular centerpiece for a Christmas dinner.

suckling pig (about 12 lbs.)*
cranberries, a small apple,
and watercress or parsley for
garnishing

oil and butter

Thread a long spit through the pig's mouth and stomach cavity, and fasten securely with skewers and by tying front and hind legs together with butcher's twine. This may take some doing, but be sure the pig is well secured, so that it rotates with the spit when the spit is turned. Cover ears and tail with foil, and wedge a block of wood in the pig's mouth to keep it open. Place before a brisk fire to roast. Since a pig extended full length is rather long, it will be necessary to build a larger-than-usual, or double, fire for cooking. For instructions on how to do this, see Chapter 2, The Cooking Fire. Place a large dripping pan under the pig, and 2 reflecting panels in front of it to intensify the fire's heat and to reflect it onto the side of the pig not facing the fire. Let the pig cook, turning it frequently, and basting it with a mixture of half melted butter and half oil. As the pig cooks, it may be necessary to cover its belly with foil, since this section will be cooked before the thicker head and hindquarters are done. The pig is done when a meat thermometer reading in its thickest part is at 180 degrees.

To serve: remove skewers, spit, foil, and wood wedge. Garnish pig by placing cranberries in eye sockets, an apple in mouth, and a wreath of parsley or watercress around neck.

Serves: 8.

Hearth Equipment: large spit. Use one made expressly for fireplace cooking by a blacksmith, as described in the Spit Roasting section of the Roasting chapter, or rent a professional electric barbecue spit from a party supplier.

Heat: high, then moderate.

Approximate Roasting Time: 3 1/2 hours or more, depending on size of pig.

Fireplace Tip: If you wish to stuff pig use a dry stuffing, such as a mixture of rice, nuts, and fruits. Just remember, it takes longer to roast a stuffed pig than an unstuffed one.

* *Suckling pigs are available through ethnic butchers, especially German and Italian, in big cities, or from a local farmer.*

Filet Mignon Steaks

6 filet mignon steaks	salt and freshly ground
6 fresh oysters	black pepper
	6 or more strips of bacon

Make a small slit with a sharp knife in one side of each steak in thickest part. Stuff one freshly shucked oyster in each pocket and season with salt and freshly ground black pepper. Wrap steaks in strips of bacon and broil over coals on gridiron until done to your taste, turning once.

Serves: 6.

Hearth Equipment: gridiron; or rotating broiler; or folding barbecue grill supported on two firebricks.

Heat: high.

Approximate Baking Time: will depend on thickness of steaks and desired degree of doneness.

Fireplace Tip: Be sure to cover hearth cooking area with aluminum foil when broiling over coals.

Prime Ribs of Beef

small rib roast (2–4 ribs)	salt and freshly ground black pepper

Wipe roast with a damp paper towel and season with salt and pepper. Pass the spit for the tin kitchen (reflector roasting oven) through the roast and secure the meat with skewers. Insert a meat thermometer into the thickest part of the roast, being careful the thermometer stem doesn't touch the bone or the spit. Insert the spitted meat into the oven and place directly in front of the fire. Roast at a high temperature for the first 15 minutes, turning the spit often to sear the meat on all sides. Lower the heat to moderate, and continue cooking until the meat is done to your taste. Basting is not necessary. Rare is 140 degrees on the meat thermometer. When done, let roast cool slightly before carving to allow the juices to retreat.

Serves: 2 persons per rib.

Hearth Equipment: tin kitchen (reflector roasting oven) or free-standing spit with improvised reflecting panels and dripping pan.

Heat: high to sear outside of roast; moderate to complete cooking.

Approximate Roasting Time: 25 minutes per pound or about 1 hour for a rare 2 1/2 pound roast.

Fireplace Tip: About 1/2 hour before roast is completed, one can pour off drippings and use to make your favorite Yorkshire pudding recipe in Dutch oven.

Cornish Hens

4 rock Cornish hens	4 tsp. dried tarragon
salt and freshly ground black pepper	1/4 lb. butter
4 garlic cloves	1/2 cup dry white wine*

Season hens inside and out with salt and pepper. Place 1 garlic clove and 1 tsp. tarragon inside each cavity. Melt butter in posnet and add wine to make a basting sauce. Truss hens with butcher's twine, poke spit through cavity, and secure with skewers. Roast birds before a brisk fire, basting and turning occasionally, until done. Split and serve 1/2 hen to each guest.

Serves: 6–8 depending on size of hens and appetites.
Hearth Equipment: Spit, reflecting panels, dripping pan, or tin kitchen.
Heat: moderate to high.
Approximate Roasting Time: 1 hour.

* *Use white vermouth, diluted with water by 1/2, in place of white wine.*

Chinese Duck

1 fresh or thoroughly thawed
   frozen duck (4–5 lbs.)
salt and freshly ground
   black pepper
1 scallion
ginger root, small piece
1 garlic clove
salted water*

Basting Sauce:
1/4 cup soy sauce
1/4 cup honey
1/2 cup water

Rinse duck and pat dry with paper towels. Pull and trim off as much loose fat as possible and remove neck gland with small, sharp knife. Season cavity with salt and pepper and place inside: a whole trimmed scallion, a few slices of peeled ginger root, and a whole garlic clove, peeled. Skewer duck closed. Truss and tie securely with butcher's twine, leaving a long end (about 3 yards) for suspending duck in front of the fire.

Hang duck, breast down, close to the hearth floor and to the coals. Place a large, deep, pan under the duck to catch the profuse drippings. Prick the skin frequently and brush occasionally with salted water. The duck will almost rotate by itself on the cord with an occasional nudge from the cook's fork to help it along. A metal reflecting panel can be placed in front of the duck to intensify the heat (see Roasting chapter). Colonial cooks probably didn't do this, but it is in the interest of energy conservation, and it speeds up the cooking.

Baste the duck with the Chinese sauce 1/2 hour before cooking is completed. Duck is done when skin is very crisp and a cut into the inside of the thigh reveals cooked meat.

Serves: 2–4 depending on number of accompanying dishes.
Hearth Equipment: 4 yards of butcher's twine or other stout cord, a deep

dripping pan, reflecting panels or tin kitchen (reflector roasting oven); or horizontal spit; and reflecting panels.

Heat: high.

Approximate Roasting Time: 3 1/2 hours.

Fireplace Tip: Duck may have to be turned tail down midway during cooking so that it roasts evenly. The easiest way to do this is to have one person hold the duck on a platter so that the cord by which the duck is suspended is slack. One can now easily cut the cord where it joins the duck and retie it to the trussing string on the other end.

If you've never cooked a duck before, you'll be surprised at the tremendous amount of fat rendered from one relatively small bird. Make sure you use an especially generous-sized pan to catch the drippings, since it's difficult and dangerous to empty the pan while the fat is hot and the cooking is in progress.

* *Chicken broth may be substituted for the salted water.*

Planked Shad Fillets

butter	salt and freshly ground
	black pepper
2 shad fillets	parsley
lemon wedges	

Melt butter in posnet and lightly brush shad fillets on both sides. Secure fillets to plank, skin side down, around perimeter with nails. Just barely hammer nails into board for easy removal when cooking is completed. Season fillets with salt and pepper to taste, and prop before a brisk fire to cook. Turn plank halfway through cooking, so that top is now in bottom position. This will ensure that both ends of the fish cook evenly. Cook until fish flakes easily, basting with more butter if necessary, so that fish does not dry out. Do not overcook. To serve: Remove nails and garnish plank with parsley and lemon wedges.

Serves: 2.

Hearth Equipment: posnet or saucepan on a trivet. Clean hardwood board (oak or maple a good choice) or softwood board covered with foil, either must be large enough to accommodate the fillets. Nails, about a dozen, common, clean, with or without heads, of medium thickness, and at least 1 inch long.

Heat: moderate to high.

Approximate Planking Time: 10 minutes, but it will vary with the thickness of the fish.

Fireplace Tip: Save the plank and nails so that the next time you wish to plank a fish you won't have to scrounge around for these items.

Stuffed Sea Bass

1 whole sea bass* (1 1/2–2 lbs.)	1/4 tsp. salt
3 strips bacon	dash of freshly ground
	black pepper
1 cup fresh bread crumbs	1/4 tsp. marjoram
1 egg yolk	1/8 tsp. mace

Clean fish, leaving head and tail on, rinse well. Mince 1 bacon strip and sauté in spider. Toss with bread crumbs, egg yolk, salt, pepper, marjoram, and mace. Stuff fish cavity with mixture, and sew or skewer closed. Wrap outside of fish with remaining bacon.

Cook fish by planking it on a board, turning over and retying when side of fish exposed to fire flakes when pierced with fork or knife tip.

Serves: 2.

Hearth Equipment: spider or small frying pan on a trivet for sautéing bacon; planking board, butcher's twine, and aluminum foil; or fish grill.

Heat: moderate.

Approximate Planking Time: 20 minutes each side.

Fireplace Tips: To attach a whole fish to the plank, tie to board with butcher's twine, placing a thick roll of foil on either side of fish. The foil rolls brace the fish and relieve the tension of the taut string, preventing it from cutting into its tender flesh.

Always prop a whole stuffed fish in a horizontal position in front of the fire, cavity opening up, so stuffing doesn't fall out as it cooks. To serve fish right on board, remove string and foil and garnish with parsley, lemon wedges, and vegetables.

* *Other fish could be substituted, such as red snapper, or whatever is fresh that day at your fish store.*

———————————————■●◆●■———————————————

Yankee Baked Beans

1 lb. or 2 cups dried	1 tsp. dry mustard
beans: pea, marrow,	1 tsp. salt
Great Northern, lima,	1 tbsp. cider vinegar
or navy beans	1/4 tsp. ground cloves
1/2 cup molasses	1 large onion
1/4 cup brown sugar	1/2 lb. salt pork

In your kitchen: Rinse beans and pick over. Place in large saucepan with 2 qts. of water. Bring to a boil, and boil 2 minutes. Remove from heat and cover loosely. Allow to stand 1 hour. Bring to boil again; simmer gently over low heat for 1 hour or until beans are tender. Drain, reserving liquid.

Place beans in 2 1/2-quart casserole with lid. Combine 1 cup reserved liquid, molasses, brown sugar, dry mustard, salt, vinegar, cloves, and onion (chopped); stir well into beans. Score salt pork, almost but not quite through, in 1/2-inch squares. Bury in center of beans. Add enough reserved liquid to cover beans.

At the fireplace: Preheat Dutch oven with rack. Cover casserole and place on rack in preheated oven to bake slowly until beans are tender—3–5 hours may be needed. Add more reserved liquid if necessary. To give a nice glaze to the beans, during last 1/2 hour of cooking remove the casserole cover and bring salt pork to the top.

Serves: 4–6.

Hearth Equipment: Dutch oven with rack.

Heat: moderate to low.

Approximate Baking Time: 3–5 hours.

Fireplace Tip: Make sure casserole with lid will fit in Dutch oven on rack before preheating it.

Scalloped Potatoes

4–6 potatoes	2 cups light cream
1 small onion	1 tsp. salt
3 tbsp. butter	1/2 tsp. white pepper
1 1/2 tbsp. flour	1/2 tsp. dill weed

Preheat Dutch oven with rack.

Peel and thinly slice potatoes and place them in a small greased casserole or soufflé dish. Mince onion and sauté in melted butter in posnet until tender. Sprinkle onions with flour and stir together, cooking flour slightly. Add cream and seasonings, reserving some dill weed, and blend well. Bring mixture to a boil, stirring constantly with a wisk to make a smooth sauce. Pour over potatoes, lifting slices gently so sauce can seep to bottom.

Place casserole on rack in preheated oven and bake until potatoes are tender, adding more coals to top of oven near end of baking to nicely brown top of casserole. When cooked, sprinkle with dill weed and serve.

Serves: 4–6.

Hearth Equipment: posnet or saucepan on a trivet, Dutch oven on rack.

Heat: moderate.

Approximate Baking Time: 1–1 1/2 hours.

Herb Stuffed Tomatoes

4 medium to large,
   firm, ripe tomatoes
1 cup fresh bread crumbs*
2 tbsp. olive oil
1 tsp. thyme

1 tsp. basil
1 tbsp. lemon juice
1 tsp. salt
1/4 tsp. freshly ground
   black pepper
1/4 cup parmesan cheese

Preheat Dutch oven with rack.

Slice tops off tomatoes. Scoop out centers and discard seeds and juice, but reserve pulp. Chop pulp and toss with bread crumbs, oil, herbs, lemon juice, salt, and pepper. Fill tomato shells with mixture and place in oiled baking pan. Sprinkle tops with grated parmesan cheese and drizzle with a little more oil. Place pan on rack in preheated oven and bake until tomatoes are heated through and lightly browned.

Serves: 4.

Hearth Equipment: Dutch oven with rack.

Heat: moderate. Place more coals on lid of oven near the end of baking to brown cheese.

Approximate Baking Time: 20 minutes.

* *1 cup cooked rice could be substituted for bread crumbs.*

Yam Pie

Usually a dessert pie, we've reduced the sugar in this Southern specialty to make it a vegetable accompaniment. It's delicious with roast pork, chicken, etc.

2 lbs. fresh yams
3/4 cup softened butter
3 eggs
2 tbsp. brown sugar

1/2 tsp. baking powder
1 tsp. vanilla
1/4 tsp. nutmeg
1/2 tsp. cinnamon
1 unbaked 9-inch
   pie shell

Boil yams in gypsy kettle, skins on, until tender. Remove from water. Preheat Dutch oven with rack. When cool enough to handle, peel yams and mash in bowl with softened butter. Add eggs, sugar, baking powder, vanilla, and spices; mix well. Place pie shell on rack in preheated oven. Pour in yam filling, smoothing off top with a spatula. Decorate*, if desired, and bake until knife inserted in center comes out clean.

Serves: 6–8.

Hearth Equipment: gypsy kettle and Dutch oven with rack.

Heat: Boiling: high. Baking: moderate.

Approximate Baking Time: 30 minutes.

* *Leftover pastry trimmings can be used to decorate top of pie. For Thanksgiving, cut pumpkins and leaves from dough. For birthdays, the celebrant's initials or age are a festive touch.*

Breads, Muffins, and Biscuits

French Toast

2 eggs
1/8 cup milk*
1/2 tsp. vanilla

4 slices of white
or French bread

Preheat hanging griddle.

In a flat dish or pan, beat eggs, then add milk and vanilla, mixing well. Dip bread slices (cut in half if large) in this mixture, turning to coat both sides. Lightly grease hanging griddle and cook soaked slices until nicely browned on both sides. (Turn once with a spatula.) Serve with jelly, cinnamon sugar, powdered sugar, or maple syrup.

Serves: 2.

Hearth Equipment: hanging griddle, spider, or medium-sized frying pan on a trivet.
Heat: moderate to high.
Approximate Cooking Time: 2 minutes each side.

* *For a richer version, use light cream or half-and-half instead of milk.*

Bannocks

An oatmeal pancake of Scottish origin, popular in early America.

2 cups rolled oats
1 tsp. salt
1 tsp. baking soda

1 cup buttermilk or sour milk*
1 tbsp. bacon fat or
 butter, melted
1 tbsp. maple syrup
2 eggs

Preheat hanging griddle.

Combine oats, salt, and baking soda in bowl. Stir in the buttermilk, bacon fat, and maple syrup. Lightly beat eggs and add, mixing all ingredients together thoroughly.

Grease griddle and place spoonfuls of batter on it and bake, turning Bannocks once with a spatula.

Serves: 4.

Hearth Equipment: hanging griddle, spider, or frying pan on a trivet.

Heat: moderate to high.

Approximate Baking Time: 3–4 minutes on each side.

* *To sour milk: add 1 tsp. lemon juice or vinegar to 1 cup of milk. Let sit 10 minutes.*

Perfect Corn Bread

This is the simplest of all Dutch oven recipes, and a good choice for your first attempt at fireplace baking.

1 cup sifted flour
1/4 cup sugar
4 tsp. baking powder
3/4 tsp. salt

1 cup yellow cornmeal
1/4 cup shortening, butter
 or margarine
1 cup milk
2 eggs
fresh maple leaves
 with stems*

Preheat Dutch oven.

Combine and sift the flour, sugar, baking powder, and salt into a bowl; add cornmeal and mix. Melt shortening in spider and add to dry ingredients.

* *Two thicknesses of heavy brown paper (grease top layer) cut to fit bottom of Dutch oven could be used in place of the fresh maple leaves.*

Lightly beat milk and eggs together. Mix thoroughly with dry ingredients, but do not overbeat.

Carefully, so as not to burn fingers, line the preheated oven with maple leaves. Then pour the corn bread mixture over them and bake until a cake tester or toothpick inserted in center comes out clean.

Cool corn bread slightly in Dutch oven and turn out onto a wooden cutting board. Gently pull off the maple leaves, using their stems as handles. They will leave a pretty pattern on the finished bread. Cut into wedges and serve.

Serves: 6–8.

Hearth Equipment: spider, posnet or small saucepan on a trivet; Dutch oven.

Heat: melting, low; baking, moderate to high. Pile slightly more coals on lid of oven near end of baking to brown top crust of corn bread.

Approximate Baking Time: 20 minutes.

Fireplace Tip: This recipe is especially fun to do with children. Let the youngest ones gather the maple leaves while the older ones mix the batter.

Jalapeno Corn Bread

1/2 lb. bacon	1/2 cup cornmeal
1 small onion	1 egg
1/2 cup flour	3 tbsp. butter
3 tsp. baking powder	3/4 cup buttermilk
1 tsp. salt	1 cup canned corn niblets
2 tsp. sugar	1/3 cup canned green chilies

Sauté bacon until crisp in spider. Drain and crumble. Pour off most of the drippings and reserve. Chop onion and sauté in remaining fat in spider. Sift together flour, baking powder, salt, and sugar into a bowl. Stir in cornmeal. Beat egg slightly, and melt butter in large spoon over coals. Mix butter and egg with buttermilk. Add to flour mixture, and blend. Add corn niblets (well drained), bacon, onions, and chilies (well drained), and mix until just blended. Heat 3 tbsp. of the reserved bacon fat in the spider; pour in batter. Cover spider with a lid and bake over coals until done, when a cake-tester or toothpick inserted in center comes out clean. Cool slightly, and serve while still warm, cut in wedges.

Serves: 6.

Hearth Equipment: spider with improvised lid or Dutch oven with lid.

Heat: hot.

Approximate Baking Time: 20 minutes.

Anadama Bread

According to American folklore, a frustrated frontier husband, weary of his wife's daily cornmeal mush, invented this recipe. One night after a hard day in the field, he flew into a rage when confronted with the usual fare. Deciding to take things into his own hands, he mixed up this instead—muttering all the while, "Anna, damn her!"

1 1/2 cups water	1 pkg. dry yeast
1 tsp. salt	1/4 cup water
1/3 cup yellow cornmeal	4 1/2 cups flour
1/3 cup molasses	fresh maple leaves
1 1/2 tbsp. butter	with stems*
	1 tbsp. vinegar

In your kitchen: Bring 1 1/2 cups water to boil in a saucepan, stir in salt and cornmeal. Stirring constantly, bring to a second boil. Remove from heat and pour into a large bowl. Stir in molasses and butter and cool to lukewarm. Sprinkle yeast on 1/4 cup lukewarm water to dissolve. Blend into cornmeal mixture with flour. Knead well. Let the dough rise in a greased bowl, covered, until double in bulk, about 1 1/2 hours.

At the fireplace: Preheat Dutch oven. Punch down dough and form into a round loaf. Line preheated oven with maple leaves and sprinkle with cornmeal. Brush top of bread with vinegar and place in oven to bake until bread is nicely browned and sounds hollow when top is tapped with knuckles.

Yield: 1 large loaf.

Hearth Equipment: Dutch oven.

Heat: moderate to high.

Approximate Baking Time: 45 minutes.

Fireplace Tip: The hearth is a good place to allow yeast breads to rise. But don't place them too close to the fire or its embers, as too intense a heat will kill the growing yeast.

* *Two thicknesses of heavy brown paper cut to fit bottom of Dutch oven could be used in place of the fresh maple leaves.*

Oatmeal Bread

1 cup milk	1/4 cup lukewarm water
1/2 cup shortening (1/2 butter)	4 cups sifted flour
1/4 cup sugar	2 cups rolled oats
1 1/2 tsp. salt	2 eggs
1 pkg. dry yeast	cinnamon
	melted butter

Scald milk in spider and stir in shortening, sugar, and salt. Cool mixture to lukewarm. Sprinkle yeast over 1/4 cup lukewarm water to soften. In large bowl place 1 cup flour and oats. Stir in milk mixture, lightly beaten eggs, and yeast. Add remaining flour and mix well. Turn dough onto a floured cloth and knead until smooth and elastic. Place in a greased bowl and grease top. (Turn dough over in bowl a few times.) Cover and let rise until double in bulk, about 1 1/2 hours.

Punch dough down, turn onto floured cloth, and let rest 10 minutes. Divide dough in half. Roll each half into a rectangle and lightly dust with cinnamon. Re-roll and put each coil into a greased round cake pan or individual bread loaf pans. Let rise until double in bulk, about 1/2 hour.

Preheat Dutch oven, with rack. Melt butter in spider. Brush tops of loaves with melted butter and bake separately in oven until done (when a hollow sound is heard when the tops of the breads are rapped with knuckles).

Yield: 2 loaves.

Hearth Equipment: spider or saucepan on a trivet; Dutch oven.

Heat: for scalding milk, high; for melting butter, low; for baking bread, moderate to hot. During latter part of baking, pile slightly more coals on lid of oven to brown top crust of bread.

Approximate Baking Time: 40 minutes.

Fireplace Tips: The hearth is a fine place to allow yeast breads to rise. But don't place them too close to the fire or its embers, as too intense a heat will kill the growing yeast. Both loaves could be baked at once in two stacked Dutch ovens or on leaves as described in the Baking chapter under alternate uses of the Dutch oven.

Fragrant Herb Bread

2 pkgs. dry yeast	1 cup lukewarm water
1/2 cup lukewarm water	1/4 cup olive oil
pinch of sugar	1 tbsp. dried sage, parsley,
4 cups of flour	or dill weed
2 tsp. salt	heavy brown paper
	coarse salt

Dissolve yeast in 1/2 cup lukewarm water with a pinch of sugar. In a large bowl, combine flour and salt. Make a well in center of flour, and add dissolved yeast mixture and cup of lukewarm water. Allow flour to gradually work into the dough, stirring gently. Transfer mixture to a floured board and knead until smooth and satiny. Add more flour if necessary. Form into a ball. Place in bowl which has been oiled. Cover and let rise in warm place until double in bulk, about 1 hour.

Punch down dough. Work in 1/4 cup olive oil and herbs. Knead until smooth. Roll out 1/2 dough on 2 thicknesses of oiled brown paper cut to fit bottom of Dutch oven. Repeat with other 1/2 of dough. (Dough may be patted and pulled by hand instead of using a rolling pin.) Allow to rise, covered until double in bulk. About 45 minutes.

Preheat Dutch oven. Prick bread in 5–6 places with fork. Sprinkle lightly with coarse salt. Place first loaf of bread, paper and all, in oven to bake. Keep second loaf out of draft, but not too close to the heat. Bake when first is done.

Yield: 2 loaves.

Hearth Equipment: Dutch oven.

Heat: moderate to high. Pile slightly more coals on lid of oven near end of baking to ensure nicely browned top crust.

Approximate Baking Time: 25 minutes per loaf.

Fireplace Tip: Cut brown paper circles to fit Dutch oven bottom before preheating it!

The hearth is a fine place to allow yeast breads to rise. Don't place them too close to the fire or its embers, as too intense a heat will kill the growing yeast.

Both loaves could be baked at once in two stacked Dutch ovens, as described in the Baking chapter under alternate uses of the Dutch oven.

Steamed Boston Brown Bread

1/2 cup flour	1/2 cup yellow cornmeal
1/2 tsp. baking soda	1/2 cup whole wheat flour
1/2 tsp. salt	1 cup sour milk*
1 tsp. cinnamon	1/4 cup molasses
2 tbsp. sugar	1/2 cup raisins

Sift together flour, baking soda, salt, and cinnamon. Stir in sugar, corn-meal, and whole wheat flour. Add milk, molasses, and raisins, stirring until just blended. Pour into a well-greased, 1-pound coffee can or mold which is lined with a circle of greased waxed paper at the bottom. Cover can with greased waxed paper or aluminum foil and tie securely with string.

Place can on a rack in a gypsy kettle. Add *boiling* water to reach halfway up the side of the can. Cover kettle and steam about 3 hours, replenishing the water as necessary if it boils away. (Always add boiling water.) When done, the bread will have risen and a cake-tester inserted in center will come out clean. Remove bread from can while still hot. Serve warm with butter or cream cheese.

Yield: 1 loaf.
Hearth Equipment: gypsy kettle with rack.
Heat: high.
Approximate Steaming Time: 3 hours.
Fireplace Tip: Keep a filled teakettle on the hearth so boiling water is readily available.

* *To sour milk: add 1 tsp. lemon juice or vinegar to 1 cup of milk. Let sit 10 minutes.*

Sweet Potato Buns

1/2 pkg. dry yeast	1 tsp. salt
1/2 cup warm water	1 cup mashed sweet potato
1 cup milk	2 eggs
2/3 cup butter	6 cups flour
1/2 cup sugar	1/4 tsp. cardamom

Sprinkle yeast on warm water, stir to dissolve. Scald milk in spider and add butter, sugar, salt, and sweet potatoes. Mix well and cool to lukewarm. Stir in dissolved yeast, eggs, flour, and cardamom. Knead on a floured board until smooth and satiny. Place in greased bowl. Cover and let rise until doubled in bulk in a warm place. Punch down and allow dough to rest, covered, for 5 minutes. Divide dough in half, shape each half into 9 buns, and place them in two greased 8-inch-square pans. Do not allow buns to touch. During the next rising they will meet and can be pulled apart when baked to serve. Cover and let rise until doubled in bulk. Bake buns, one pan at a time, on rack in preheated Dutch oven.

Yield: 1 1/2 dozen.
Hearth Equipment: spider; Dutch oven with rack.
Heat: for scalding milk, high; for baking buns, moderate to high.

Approximate Baking Time: 20–30 minutes.

Fireplace Tips: The hearth is a good place to allow yeast breads to rise: But don't place them too close to the fire or its embers, as too intense a heat will kill the growing yeast.

Both pans of buns could be baked at once in 2 stacked Dutch ovens, as described in the Baking chapter under alternate uses of the Dutch oven.

Cornmeal Biscuits

1/3 cup cracklings*
1 1/2 cups any biscuit
   mix
1/2 cup cornmeal

2/3 cup light cream
shortening to grease griddle

Render pork rind or fat in spider to make cracklings. Preheat hanging griddle. Blend biscuit mix, cornmeal, cracklings, and light cream in a bowl with a fork until it forms a soft dough. Knead 10–12 times on a lightly floured board. Roll dough 1/4-inch thick. Cut with a floured 1–1 1/2-inch cutter. Lightly grease preheated griddle, wiping off any "pools" of melted shortening. Place half the biscuits on the griddle and bake until they have risen and are a delicate brown on one side. Turn and brown on other side. Remove and bake remaining biscuits.

Yield: 1 1/2 dozen biscuits.

Hearth Equipment: spider or frying pan on a trivet; hanging griddle or reflector bake oven.

Heat: for rendering, high; for baking, moderate to high.

Approximate Baking Time: 5–7 minutes each side.

* *Crumbled bacon could be substituted.*

English Muffins

1 pkg. dry yeast
1/4 cup lukewarm water
1 cup milk
2 tbsp. sugar
1 1/2 tsp. salt

3 tbsp. shortening
4 cups flour
1 egg, lightly beaten
cornmeal

Soften yeast in water. Scald milk in spider, add sugar, salt, and shortening. Cool to lukewarm and pour into large bowl. Add 2 cups of flour and mix well. Add yeast and egg, and beat in enough of the remaining 2 cups of flour to make a moderately soft dough. Knead until smooth and satiny. Place in a greased bowl, greasing the top by turning it once or twice in the prepared bowl. Cover with a dish towel or Saran Wrap, and let rise until double in bulk, about 1 hour.

Punch down and roll 1/4-inch thick, and cut into 3-inch circles with a floured metal cutter or a drinking glass. Let the individual biscuits rise again until they are double in bulk, about 45 minutes.

Preheat griddle. (A drop of water should dance on it.) Sprinkle with cornmeal and place biscuits on it to bake. When they have browned nicely on one side, turn, adding more cornmeal to the griddle, if necessary.

Yield: 1 dozen 3-inch muffins.

Hearth Equipment: spider or saucepan on a trivet; hanging griddle, reflector bake oven, or frying pan on a trivet.

Heat: for scalding, high; for baking, moderate.

Approximate Baking Time: 8–10 minutes each side.

Fireplace Tip: The warm hearth area is a good place for dough and muffins to rise. But don't place them too close to the fire or its embers, as too intense a heat will kill the growing yeast.

The finished muffins can be toasted at the hearth, as well. Just split or tear them apart with fingers or a fork, and toast either in a traditional down-hearth toaster or on the end of a long-handled fork.

Desserts:
Cakes, Cookies, Pies, and Puddings

Apple Coffee Cake

1/2 cup butter	1 tsp. cinnamon
1 cup sugar	3/4 tsp. ground cloves
2 eggs	1/2 cup cold, black coffee
1 1/2 cups flour	2 cups peeled, shredded apple
1 tsp. baking soda	1 cup raisins
3/4 tsp. salt	1/2 cup broken walnuts

Preheat Dutch oven with rack.

Cream butter with sugar. Add eggs and beat until fluffy. Sift together dry ingredients and add alternately with coffee to creamed mixture, beginning and ending with dry ingredients. Mix in apple, raisins, and walnuts.

Pour cake batter into a greased and floured 9-x-2-inch round pan. Place on rack in preheated oven and bake until a cake-tester or toothpick inserted in center comes out clean.

Serves: 6–8.

Hearth Equipment: Dutch oven with rack.

Heat: moderate.

Approximate Baking Time: 1 hour, 15 minutes.

Blueberry Cake

1/3 cup butter	1/8 tsp. cinnamon
1 cup sugar	1/2 cup sour milk*
1 egg	or buttermilk
2 cups flour	2 1/2 cups frozen blueberries**
1 tsp. baking soda	

Preheat Dutch oven with rack.

Cream the butter until light, then add the sugar and continue creaming until fluffy. Beat in egg. Sift together flour, soda, and cinnamon. Add alternately with the sour milk to the creamed mixture, beginning and ending with the dry ingredients. The batter will be stiff, but it must be, to support the weight of the blueberries now to be added.

Pick over berries, discarding stems and any green or withered ones, but do not defrost. Stir into batter and spread in a well-greased 9-x-9-x-2-inch square or a deep 9-inch round pan. Place cake in preheated oven on a rack, and bake until a cake-tester or toothpick inserted in center comes out clean.

Serves: 6–8.

Hearth Equipment: Dutch oven with rack.

Heat: moderate.

Approximate Baking Time: 50–60 minutes.

* *To sour milk: Add 1 tsp. lemon juice or vinegar to 1 cup of milk. Let sit 10 minutes.*
** *Fresh blueberries are better in this cake, but it is unlikely that you will find them in the market during fireplace cooking weather.*

Carrot Cake

1/2 cup butter	1 tsp. salt
1 1/2 cups brown sugar	2 tsp. cinnamon
3 eggs	1/4 tsp. freshly grated nutmeg
Enough carrots to equal	1/2 tsp. cardamom
2 cups when grated	1 cup walnuts
2 cups flour	1 cup coconut
2 tsp. baking soda	1/2 cup raisins
2 tsp. baking powder	

Preheat Dutch oven with rack.

Cream butter and sugar together. Separate eggs, and beat in yolks. Grate carrots and add. Mix well, and let stand a few minutes.

Sift together flour, baking soda, baking powder, salt, and spices. Combine with carrot mixture. Beat egg whites until stiff. Break walnuts into pieces.

Gently fold egg whites into batter with coconut, nuts, and raisins. Place greased and floured tube or Bundt pan on rack in preheated oven. Put cake mixture into it, and bake until a cake-tester or toothpick inserted in center comes out clean.

Serves: 8.

Hearth Equipment: Dutch oven with rack.
Heat: moderate.
Approximate Baking Time: 1 hour.
Fireplace Tip: Make sure baking pan fits into Dutch oven before attempting to fill it. Try pans in cold oven before beginning recipe.

Gingerbread

1/2 cup sugar	1 egg
1/2 cup butter	3/4 cup dark molasses
1 tsp. ginger	1 cup sour milk*
1 tsp. cinnamon	2 cups flour
1/2 tsp. salt	1 tsp. baking soda

Preheat Dutch oven with rack.

Cream sugar, butter, ginger, cinnamon, and salt together. Add egg and beat until fluffy. Mix in molasses and milk. Sift together flour and baking soda. Add, mixing batter until smooth.

Place a greased and floured 9-inch square pan on rack in preheated oven and pour gingerbread mixture into it. Bake until top of cake springs back when touched with your finger. Cut into squares when cool. Great with whipped cream or vanilla ice cream!

Serves: 8 or more, depending on size of squares.

Hearth Equipment: Dutch oven with rack.
Heat: moderate. Pile slightly more coals on top of oven near end of baking to brown top of gingerbread.
Approximate Baking Time: 30–40 minutes.

* *To sour milk: Add 1 tsp. lemon juice or vinegar to 1 cup of milk. Let sit 10 minutes.*

Brownies

2 squares of unsweetened
  chocolate
1/3 cup butter
1 cup sugar
2 eggs

3/4 cup sifted flour
1/2 tsp. baking powder
1/2 tsp. salt
1/2 cup walnuts

Preheat Dutch oven with rack.

Melt chocolate and butter in a spider and stir in sugar and eggs. Sift together flour, baking powder, and salt, and add to chocolate mixture. Break walnuts into pieces and stir into batter. Pour mixture into greased and floured* 8-inch square pan and place on rack in oven. Bake until cake-tester or toothpick inserted in center comes out clean. Let cool slightly and cut into 16 squares.

Hearth Equipment: Dutch oven with rack.

Heat: moderate.

Approximate Baking Time: 30–35 minutes.

* *Dusting pan with cocoa instead of flour works just as well, and it is a more compatible color with the brownie batter.*

Springerle Cookies

4 eggs
1 lb. confectioner's
  sugar
4 1/2 cups cake flour

1 tsp. baking powder
1 tbsp. grated lemon rind
anise seed

In your kitchen: In large bowl of electric mixer, beat eggs at medium speed. Gradually add confectioner's sugar and continue beating until thoroughly mixed. Sift together flour and baking powder, add with grated lemon rind to egg mixture, and mix well. Wrap dough, and refrigerate 1 hour. Generously grease 2 large cookie sheets and sprinkle with anise seed. Roll dough 1/2-inch thick on floured surface. With a floured Springerle Board, print and cut shapes with knife. Put cookies on prepared sheets and let stand about 12 hours (overnight) at room temperature. This is to let cookies dry out sufficiently, so that they will retain their shape and detail when baked.

At your fireplace: Bake cookies in reflector oven until lightly browned.

Yield: will depend on size of mold.

Hearth Equipment: reflector bake oven or Dutch oven with foil-covered rack to make improvised cookie sheet.

Approximate Baking Time: 30 minutes.

Fireplace Tips: Make the dough first thing in the morning and cookies will be ready for baking at dinner time.

Waffles

1 cup flour	4 eggs
1 tsp. baking powder	1/3 cup sugar
1 tsp. cinnamon	1 cup sour cream
1/4 cup butter	

Sift together flour, baking powder, and cinnamon. Beat eggs and sugar until thick and lemon-colored. Fold flour mixture into beaten eggs alternately with sour cream. Melt butter in spider and stir into batter.

Preheat waffle iron, which has been seasoned with vegetable shortening. Pour in waffle batter and bake until iron no longer steams and edges of waffle appear golden brown.

Yield: 4 waffles.

Hearth Equipment: spider or saucepan on a trivet; waffle iron.

Heat: for melting butter, low; for baking waffles, moderate to high.

Approximate Baking Time: 2 minutes per waffle.

Fireplace Tip: Waffle iron may have to be reseasoned if a large batch is made; you'll know when it's time, as waffles start to stick! Just reseason iron by applying a little more shortening and heating. Recipe on Bisquick box works well, too.

Wafers

1/2 cup butter	2 1/4 cups flour
3 eggs	1/2 tsp. grated lemon rind or
1 cup sugar	1 tsp. mace

Melt butter in spider and allow to cool slightly. Beat eggs and sugar together until light and fluffy. Stir in melted butter, flour, and grated lemon rind or mace.

Form balls* from the dough using about 1 tbsp. for each wafer. Place on a preheated and lightly oiled wafer iron. Close iron and cook wafer until steam stops. Remove wafer from iron, curling it up, if you wish, for filling later, or leaving it flat to be served as a cookie. Serve filled or topped with whipped cream, ice cream, preserves, etc. Use your imagination!

Yield: The number will depend on the size of your iron, but a few dozen, at least.

Hearth Equipment: wafer iron or Pizzelle iron.

Heat: Drops of water should dance on the hot iron baking surface.

Approximate Baking Time: 2 minutes.

* *If your wafer iron is rectangular, roll the dough into a finger to make a complete wafer on your iron.*

S'mores

An old Girl Scout campfire favorite and great for a child's party. The guests can even make these themselves!

8 whole graham crackers	8 large marshmallows
4 small chocolate bars	

Break graham crackers in half so that you have 16 squares. Place 8 of the squares in a reflector bake oven and top each with a marshmallow. Place oven in front of fire and bake until marshmallows are gooey and slightly browned. Remove and place half a chocolate bar on each marshmallow. Top with another graham cracker square, pressing down lightly to complete the dessert sandwich.

Yield: 8, but everyone always wants *s'more.*
Hearth Equipment: reflector baking oven.
Heat: moderate.
Approximate Baking Time: 2–3 minutes.
Fireplace Tip: The marshmallow can also be melted on long-handled forks held before the fire and then just squished between the crackers with the chocolate.

* *For a variation, spread peanut butter on graham crackers.*

Apple Pie

2/3 cup sugar	1/2 tsp. cinnamon
1 tbsp. flour	2 1/2 lbs. cooking apples
1/8 tsp. salt	juice of 1 lemon
1/2 tsp. grated lemon rind	1 tbsp. butter
1/4 tsp. freshly grated	pastry for a two crust,
nutmeg	9-inch pie
	egg wash*

Preheat Dutch oven with rack.

Combine sugar, flour, salt, lemon rind, nutmeg, and cinnamon in a small dish. Core, peel, and slice apples, and toss with lemon juice to keep from discoloring.

Assemble pie: Line pie plate with pastry dough and sprinkle bottom with 3 tablespoons of the sugar mixture. Toss apples with remaining sugar and add to pie shell. Dot with butter. Paint egg wash on edges of bottom crust to create a good seal, and cover with top crust. Trim and crimp edges of pie attractively, making slits in top for steam to escape. Brush with remaining egg wash.

Bake on a rack in preheated oven until top crust is golden brown and apples are tender.

Serves: 8.

Hearth Equipment: Dutch oven with rack.

Heat: moderate to high. For first 15 minutes of baking, pile slightly more coals under Dutch oven to set bottom crust. Last 15 minutes, pile slightly more coals on top of oven to brown top crust.

Approximate Baking Time: 40 minutes.

Fireplace Tip: Pass a plate of cheese slices with the pie. Guests can add these themselves and melt them by passing an ember held with tongs over their own servings.

* *To make egg wash: Stir together 1 lightly beaten egg with 1 tsp. water.*

Pecan Pie

4 eggs	1 tbsp. butter
3/4 cup sugar	1 tsp. vanilla extract
1/2 tsp. salt	2 cups pecan pieces plus
3/4 cup light corn syrup	10–12 unbroken halves*
	1 unbaked 9-inch pie shell

Preheat Dutch oven with rack.

Beat eggs lightly and add sugar, salt, and corn syrup. Melt tablespoon of butter in large long-handled metal spoon held over embers or near fire. Stir in melted butter and vanilla and mix well. Spread pecan pieces on bottom of pie shell and carefully place shell on rack in preheated oven. Pour egg mixture over nuts and arrange perfect pecan halves in a pattern on top of pie.

Bake pie until a cake-tester or toothpick inserted in middle comes out clean. Serve topped with whipped cream.

Serves: 8.

Hearth Equipment: Dutch oven with rack; large long-handled metal spoon.

Heat: moderate to hot. Place more coals underneath pie during first part of baking to set bottom crust.

Approximate Baking Time: 40 minutes.

Fireplace Tip: Pie shell could be a frozen one right from your freezer.

* *Wild hickory nuts can be substituted for pecan. While they are delicious, they are very difficult to shell. Almost none will be perfect enough to decorate top, so just increase overall nut pieces to 2 1/4 cups.*

Holiday Plum Pudding

3 cups coarse, fresh
  bread crumbs
1 cup milk
1/2 cup butter
1 (10 oz.) jar peach
  jam
1 cup flour

1 tsp. baking soda
1 tsp. salt
2 tsp. cinnamon
1/4 tsp. each allspice and cloves
1/2 cup broken walnuts
1/2 cup mixed, candied fruits

Place bread crumbs in a large bowl and pour milk over them. Allow to soak a few minutes. Meanwhile, melt butter in spider and stir in jam. Sift flour, soda, salt, and spices into bread crumb mixture with nuts, coarsely chopped, and candied fruits. Pour into a well-greased 1 qt. mold. Cover with aluminum foil. Secure with string or wire. Place in gypsy kettle which has rack on the bottom, and hang from crane. Add boiling water to halfway up the side of the mold. Cover kettle with a tight-fitting lid and steam until pudding tests done with a cake-tester. Add more hot water as needed to maintain water level in kettle. When done turn out onto warm serving dish and serve with hard sauce.

Serves: 10.

Hearth Equipment: gypsy kettle with rack.

Heat: moderate to high.

Approximate Steaming Time: 3 hours.

Fireplace Tip: Keep a teakettle of water boiling on the crane to replenish pudding kettle as needed to maintain water level halfway up the side of the mold.

Apricot and Apple Steamed Pudding

2 1/2 cups flour
1 tsp. salt
1 tsp. baking powder
1/2 tsp. cinnamon
1/4 tsp. nutmeg
1/4 tsp. ginger

1/4 cup butter
3/4 cup brown sugar
1 egg
1/2 cup milk
1 large shredded apple
1/2 cup dried apricots
3/4 cup walnut pieces

Sift together flour, salt, baking powder, and spices. Cream together butter and sugar. Add egg and continue creaming until well mixed. Stir in half the flour mixture. Add milk, blend. Add remaining flour and mix in. Peel and core apple and shred (it should equal 1 cup.) Slice apricots, into quarters. Stir fruit and nuts into batter. Pour pudding mixture into a 6-cup mold that has been well greased and dusted with fine bread crumbs. (An empty 2-lb. coffee can works very well.) Cover tightly with greased aluminum foil. Tie cover in place with string or wire, if it cannot be secured in any other way. Set on rack in gypsy kettle. Place kettle on crane. Add enough boiling water to come about halfway up sides of mold. Cover kettle and steam until pudding tests done with a cake-tester. To serve, remove from kettle and let stand about 10 minutes, then invert mold. Pudding should have shrunk enough for easy removal. Slice and top with hard sauce, lemon sauce or ice cream.

Serves: 8–10.
Hearth Equipment: gypsy kettle.
Heat: moderate to high.
Approximate Steaming Time: 1 1/2 hours.
Fireplace Tip: Keep a teakettle of water boiling on the crane to add to pudding kettle as needed. Water level should remain halfway up pudding mold as it cooks.

Pumpkin Pudding

4 eggs
1 large can pumpkin,
   1 lb., 13 oz.
2 tbsp. flour
2 tbsp. cornstarch
1 tsp. salt

1 tsp. cinnamon
1/2 tsp. nutmeg, freshly
   grated
1/8 tsp. cloves (optional)
1 cup honey
1 tsp. vanilla
3 cups milk*

Preheat Dutch oven with rack.

Beat eggs well, mix in pumpkin. Stir together all dry ingredients, then add to pumpkin mixture with honey, vanilla, and milk and blend in. Place empty, lightly buttered, 2-qt. casserole on rack in preheated oven and fill with pumpkin mixture. Bake until a knife inserted in center comes out clean.

Serves: 6.
Hearth Equipment: Dutch oven with rack.
Heat: moderate.
Approximate Baking Time: 1 hour.

* *Undiluted evaporated milk may be used.*

Crème Caramel

1/2 cup sugar	1/8 tsp. salt
2 cups milk	1/2 tsp. vanilla
3 eggs	grated rind of
1/4 cup sugar	1/2 small lemon

Preheat Dutch oven with rack and 1 inch of water in bottom.

Caramelize the 1/2 cup of sugar by heating it until it liquifies and turns a golden brown in a spider. Put 1 tablespoon of the caramel in each of 4 custard cups, tipping them quickly to coat bottoms.

Scald milk in the spider. Beat the eggs lightly with 1/4 cup sugar and salt in mixing bowl. Add hot milk slowly to egg mixture, stirring constantly. Strain. Mix in vanilla and lemon rind.

Place caramel-coated cups in preheated oven in water bath on rack. Fill with custard mixture. Add more *hot* water to the oven, as necessary, to reach midway up sides of custard cups. Bake gently until knife inserted in custard comes out clean. Let custard cool and serve unmolded, garnished with whipped cream and toasted, slivered almonds, if desired.

Serves: 6.

Hearth Equipment: spider or small frying pan on a trivet; Dutch oven with rack.

Heat: for caramelizing sugar, very high; for scalding milk, high; for baking custard, moderate to low (make sure that water in oven only simmers and does not boil).

Approximate Baking Time: 30–40 minutes.

Fireplace Tip: A teakettle near the fire or on the crane is a convenient source of hot water.

Sautéed Bananas

3 ripe, but still firm bananas	1/2 cup brown sugar
	1/2 cup orange juice
2 tbsp. lemon juice	1/8 tsp. cinnamon
4 tbsp. butter	

Peel bananas and slice crosswise in circles. Toss with lemon juice. Melt butter in spider. Add brown sugar and cook until melted. Add bananas and toss lightly to coat with sugar mixture. Sauté lightly, then add orange juice and cinnamon. Heat until juice is warm. Serve over butter pecan ice cream, or any other favorite flavor.

Serves: 4–6.

Hearth Equipment: spider or frying pan on a trivet.

Heat: moderate.

Approximate Cooking Time: 7–10 minutes.

Jersey Lightning Fritters

6 crisp cooking apples	1 cup beer (flat)
1 cup sugar	1 cup flour
3 tbsp. applejack	shortening
1 tbsp. lemon juice	cinnamon sugar

Peel and core apples. Slice into 1/4-inch rings. Combine sugar, applejack, and lemon juice in a shallow dish. Soak apple rings in mixture 1 hour, turning once. Whisk flat beer and flour together to make a smooth batter.*

Preheat spider with 1 inch of shortening in it. Dip apple rings in batter and fry until golden and puffed, turning them once. Drain on paper towels and serve with cinnamon sugar.

Serves: 6.

Hearth Equipment: spider or bottom of Dutch oven.

Heat: hot. Don't put too many apple rings into oil at one time, as they will lower the temperature below the frying point.

Approximate Frying Time: 3–5 minutes each side.

Fireplace Tip: Be extremely careful when frying over coals. Don't let any embers get into the oil or allow it to splatter.

* *Beer batter should rest about 1 hour before using.*

Poached Spiced Pears

6 winter pears	2 tbsp. butter
1/2 cup sugar	2 cloves
2 tbsp. lemon juice	1 piece of cinnamon stick
1 cup boiling water	6 tbsp. chocolate sauce

Preheat Dutch oven with rack. Peel pears and core from the bottom with a melon baller. Leave stem in place. Combine sugar, lemon juice, butter, water, and spices. Simmer in posnet 5 minutes. Remove cloves and cinnamon stick.

Place pears, stem up, in casserole, pour syrup over them. Place in preheated oven on rack to bake. Baste occasionally. The pears are done when they can be pierced easily with the tip of a sharp knife. Serve with 1 tablespoon of chocolate sauce drizzled over neck of each pear.

Serves: 6.

Hearth Equipment: for simmering, posnet or saucepan on a trivet; for baking, Dutch oven with rack.

Heat: for simmering, moderate to low; for baking, moderate.

Approximate Baking Time: 45 minutes.

Ember Glazed Baked Apples

A sophisticated and delicious version of the ordinary baked apple contributed by David Kimmel, a graduate and director of the Culinary Institute of America.

4 baking apples	1 cinnamon stick
(Rome beauties)	1/4 cup white wine*
1/4 cup honey	2 tbsp. brown sugar
1 tbsp. raisins	

Preheat Dutch oven with rack.

Core apples almost all the way through bottom, remove skin from top third. Place apples in baking pan and fill centers with honey and raisins. Place cinnamon stick in pan and pour wine over all.

Place pan on rack in preheated oven to bake. Baste apples occasionally with juices until done, tender but not mushy. When cooked, sprinkle apples with brown sugar and glaze by holding a hot ember with tongs or preheated salamander near the sugar.

Serves: 4.

Hearth Equipment: Dutch oven with rack; ember tongs, salamander, or metal kitchen, or barbecue tongs.

Heat: moderate.

Approximate Baking Time: 30 minutes.

Fireplace Tip: For the novice fireplace cook, this dessert can be easily prepared by simply wrapping each apple and its seasonings in several thicknesses of foil and allowing it to cook in the hot embers, Indian style. To glaze tops, open foil and proceed as directed above.

* *Use white vermouth, diluted with water by 1/2, in place of white wine.*

9

Where to Learn about Fireplace Cooking

othing quite matches the experience of learning a skill firsthand from an acknowledged expert. But since we can't bring back Eliza Leslie or Amelia Simmons to lecture on the art of fireplace cooking, we will direct you to the next best source: locations in the United States where open-hearth cooking is demonstrated and/or taught.

All the restored or re-created villages, plantations, farms, forts, and dwellings listed in this chapter demonstrate fireplace cooking as it was practiced in America's past. A variety of sites is included, ranging in period from the very early colonization of America, re-created at Plimoth Plantation, to a much later era preserved at Hancock Shaker Village. They recall a fascinating array of American ways of life, from the elegance and sophistication of Colonial Williamsburg to the simple farm setting of Old Sturbridge Village and the pioneer spirit of Missouri Town, 1855.

In general, these museums use a "living history" format to portray the life and the technology—cooking and manufacturing—of the different periods. Here, trained guides—often referred to as museum interpreters, since they reenact the normal tasks of the period at the site—can be observed dressed in period clothing cooking fireplace meals with antique implements or faithful reproductions. Foods indigenous to the region and menus reflecting the tastes and ethnic origins of its settlers are used in meal planning and preparation to create an overall effect that mirrors the past as accurately as possible.

Hamburgers, hot dogs, and steaks won't be in evidence in these fireplace kitchens, but one can get a good grasp of how to execute basic cooking techniques in a fireplace. And, using a little imagination, these skills can easily be applied to the preparation of a meal more in keeping with twentieth-century tastes.

On or near holidays, especially Thanksgiving and Christmas, many of these sites prepare more ambitious meals characteristic of the festivities and customs of the season.

Frequently the larger and better-funded sites will offer special classes or workshops in fireplace cooking, especially during the slower tourist months. A few such courses even carry college credit!

Many of the sites surveyed intend to expand or initiate fireplace cooking programs as money and popular demand increase. A good number already offer educational programs for children featuring fireplace cooking or incorporating it into a broader presentation of domestic arts from America's past. Some sites indicated their willingness to arrange workshops or classes for adults on request. Probably others could be persuaded to do so, as well. All pointed out that a major function of their cook/interpreter's role was to answer questions and discuss the history and techniques of fireplace cooking with visitors. And, when local health codes permit it, some of the cooks serve samples of their fireplace fare to the public.

We have intentionally omitted from the following descriptions details such as admission fees, hours, and dates of special events. This information is subject to change and becomes quickly outdated. We recommend, instead, that you write or call the sites that interest you for their current schedules of events, and for information on the scope of their cooking activities, as well as for any other pertinent information. Their promotional literature—brochures, calendars, maps, etc.—is usually either free or requires only a stamped, self-addressed envelope.

Do check ahead before you embark on a long trip to avoid a disappointment at your destination. It may not be apparent to a Yankee that open-hearth cooking would not be demonstrated in the deep South during the summer months, as it's just too hot!

Arizona

PIONEER ARIZONA, Interstate 17 (Pioneer Road exit), Phoenix, Arizona. (Mailing address: P.O. Box 11242, Phoenix, Arizona 85061.) Telephone: (602) 993-0210.

Pioneer Arizona is a living history museum, consisting of more than twenty-six buildings, both original and reconstructed, which depict and interpret Arizona Territory life in the late 1800's.

Fireplace cooking is demonstrated and taught here intermittently. Classes on ranch life c. 1880 currently incorporate fireplace cooking as one of their regular subjects; but this instruction is designed primarily for elementary school students and is available by advance request only.

Arkansas

ARKANSAS TERRITORIAL RESTORATION, Third and Scott Streets, Little Rock, Arkansas 72201. Telephone: (501) 371-2348.

Surrounded by contemporary buildings in center city Little Rock, the pioneer era Log House kitchen is the setting for fireplace cooking classes.

As part of the Pioneer Education Program, students (grades 6–8) can participate in the preparation and preservation of foods that were commonly available in pioneer Arkansas. Classes are limited to thirty students and must be arranged in advance.

Colorado

BENT'S OLD FORT NATIONAL HISTORIC SITE, Route 194, La Junta, Colorado (Mailing address: P.O. Box 581, La Junta, Colorado 81050.) Telephone: (303) 384-2596.

On an intermittent basis throughout the summer, fireplace cooking is demonstrated at Bent's Old Fort. A museum interpreter modeled after Black Charlotte, the fort's original cook, who was famous for her slapjacks and pumpkin pies, can be observed preparing meals and baking in the adobe ovens of the well-appointed fireplace kitchen area.

Connecticut

MYSTIC SEAPORT MUSEUM, Route 27, Mystic, Connecticut 06355. Telephone: (203) 536-2631.

Although the Mystic Seaport Museum literature describes fireplace cooking as a minor feature of the overall interpretation of Buckingham House and Mystic Seaport in general, there is an abundance of information on our subject presented here. Daily demonstrations in fireplace cooking can be observed in the kitchen of Buckingham House, a typical Connecticut dwelling of the pre-Revolutionary period. Ingredients and recipes common to the 1840's are used in meal planning and preparation.

Instruction in fireplace cooking is offered in January, February, and March. These excellent classes not only teach period techniques and recipes, but explain how to adapt this information to modern cooking implements, fireplaces, and foods. Directions for building a reflecting oven and choosing firewood, and a selection of nineteenth-century recipes, are given to the participants.

District of Columbia

OLD STONE HOUSE, 3051 M. St., N.W., Washington, D.C. 20007. Telephone: (202) 426-6851.

"The food is delicious," to quote the site manager and fireplace cook of the Old Stone House, "but unfortunately we can't give the public anything to eat, because of the D.C. Health Code."

Nevertheless, fireplace cooking can be observed in the House's well-equipped kitchen three or four times a week and at Christmastime, when a special holiday meal is prepared. Sundays, a children's program (geared for ages 10–14) includes the preparation of a typical eighteenth-century meal along with demonstrations of other early American household skills, such as spinning and quilting.

Georgia

GEORGIA AGRIRAMA, Interstate 75 and 8th St., Tifton, Georgia. (Mailing address: P.O. Box Q, Tifton, Georgia 31794.) Telephone: (912) 386-3344.

Plans are to begin fireplace cooking demonstrations and workshops in the Spring of 1980, following a research project on this topic.

Georgia Agrirama is an extensive living history museum depicting life in rural South Georgia between 1870 and 1879 through the re-creation of an operational farmstead, grist mill, saw mill, cotton gin, and historical village.

STONE MOUNTAIN ANTI-BELLUM PLANTATION, U.S. Highway 78, Stone Mountain, Georgia. (Mailing address: P.O. Box 778, Stone Mountain, Georgia 30086.) Telephone: (404) 469-9831.

Fireplace cooking can be observed every day in the cookhouse on the plantation. Typical Southern foods are prepared, which visitors are invited to sample.

The Cookhouse Sampler, published by the restoration, is for sale. It includes recipes for the foods cooked on the plantation and instructions for preparing them at the hearth, as well as in a modern kitchen.

TULLIE SMITH HOUSE RESTORATION, 3099 Andrews Drive, NW, Atlanta, Georgia. (Mailing address: P.O. Box 12423, Atlanta, Georgia 30305.) Telephone: (404) 261-1837.

Simple, hearth-baked gingerbread is prepared in the Tullie Smith House kitchen Tuesdays through Fridays from October to May. This is a favorite of the school groups which frequently visit on these days.

More elaborate, or "gourmet" fireplace cooking can be observed on Wednesday and Thursday mornings, when Kitchen Guild members prepare meals from nineteenth-century recipes.

No fireplace cooking takes place in the summer months, as it is, according to the restoration, "just too hot in Georgia!"

A cookbook, *Tullies's Receipts*, compiled by the Kitchen Guild, is available.

WESTVILLE, Route 27, Lumpkin, Georgia. (Mailing address: P.O. Box 1850, Lumpkin, Georgia 31815.) Telephone: (912) 838-6310.

Fireplace cooking, in this living history village of relocated and restored buildings that depicts the handicrafts and culture of Georgia, c. 1850, can be observed daily.

Antique implements and cooking utensils are employed to prepare a limited repertoire of foods (to date only biscuits and sausage). Small portions of the food are sold to visitors for a nominal price.

Illinois

CLAYVILLE RURAL LIFE CENTER & MUSEUM, Route 125, Pleasant Plains, Illinois. (Mailing address: R.R.1, Pleasant Plains, Illinois 62677.) Telephone: (217) 626-1132.

Fireplace cooking can be observed in the restored Clayville Inn, a farmhouse stagecoach stop originally built and operated by the Broadwell family in the 1800's. Museum interpreters cook in the Inn's fireplace, in addition to fulfilling other domestic duties, giving visitors a total picture of the daily routine of a rural, central Illinois housewife of this period.

The restoration is operated by Sangamon State University, Springfield, Illinois, and the living history presentation just described is based on substantial scholarly research.

Saturday afternoon workshops for adults in fireplace cooking have been offered in the past. And special, broader programs for school children touch on the subject, too. Museum studies and university-level courses in midwestern rural life and its regional background are conducted at Clayville, as well.

LINCOLN'S NEW SALEM, Route 97, Petersburg, Illinois. (Mailing address: Box 236, Petersburg, Illinois 62675.) Telephone: (217) 632-7953.

The generosity and interest of William Randolf Hearst, the newspaper publisher, made possible the reconstruction of New Salem as it existed in the 1830's, the years in which Abraham Lincoln spent his young adult life there.

Fireplace cooking demonstrations are presented frequently in the village, and museum interpreters use both antique and reproduction implements when preparing the food. Of the more than twenty buildings reproduced and furnished on the site, the Rutledge Tavern fireplace is especially well equipped with period cooking equipment.

At present, fireplace cooking is taught only to new help, but perhaps a particularly interested visitor might be included in these training sessions.

Indiana

THE LINCOLN LIVING HISTORICAL FARM, Lincoln Boyhood National Memorial, Indiana 162, Lincoln City, Indiana. (Mailing address: Lincoln City, Indiana 47552.) Telephone: (812) 937-4757.

The museum is on the site of the original Thomas Lincoln farm. Fireplace cooking is demonstrated at The Lincoln Living Historical Farm from the end of April through the latter part of October. These demonstrations are designed to give visitors an idea of what family and home life was like for Abraham Lincoln as he grew up on the Indiana frontier, 1816–1830.

One meal per day is prepared in the cabin fireplace by interpreters in period dress using reproductions of implements, and ingredients familiar to pioneers of this period.

Smoking meat and tapping trees for maple syrup can be observed annually.

CONNER PRAIRIE PIONEER SETTLEMENT, 30 Conner Lane, Noblesville, Indiana 46060. Telephone: (317) 773-3633.

There are six cooking fireplaces on exhibit at the Conner Prairie Pioneer Settlement, whose grounds and buildings were restored to their 1836 appearance by Eli Lilly of the pharmaceutical company. In 1964 the restoration was given to Earlham College, which now operates it as an historic landmark.

A complete fireplace meal is prepared daily in two of the fireplace kitchens of the settlement and lesser amounts of cooking can be observed in the other four hearths as well. In general, period equipment is used in these cooking demonstrations.

In the past, classes in fireplace cooking have been arranged for groups by advance request.

Iowa

LIVING HISTORY FARMS, exit 125 (Hickman Road), Interstates 35 and 80, Des Moines, Iowa. (Mailing address: Rural Route #1, Des Moines, Iowa 50322.) Telephone: (515) 278-5286.

Living History Farms is an open-air museum that encourages visitors to experience the rural life of Iowa's past through three farms: a pioneer farm of the late 1840's, a 1900's farm, and the still-developing community of Walnut Hill. Guests are invited to lend a hand as interpreters follow the daily routine of farming and domestic activities performed here.

Fireplace cooking occurs daily in two 1849 log cabins. A wide variety of open-hearth cooking techniques can be observed while the full-course meals are being prepared.

Kentucky

SHAKERTOWN AT PLEASANT HILL, U.S. Route 68, Harrodsburg, Kentucky. (Mailing address: Rte. 4, Harrodsburg, Kentucky 40330.) Telephone: (606) 734-5411.

The original Shaker Village of Pleasant Hill was established in 1805 and existed until 1910. In the 1960's it was restored to portray nineteenth-century Shaker living, and now it includes a museum village where crafts and other activities representative of Shaker life and culture are demonstrated.

Fireplace cooking and beehive oven baking are frequently included among these demonstrations. A calendar listing the dates of events at the Village is available from the restoration.

Louisiana

HERMANN–GRIMA HOUSE, 820 St. Louis Street, New Orleans, Louisiana 70112. Telephone: (504) 525-5661.

Typical nineteenth-century creole delicacies, such as King cake, gumbo, okra stew, oyster pie, corn bread, and pralines, are prepared in the kitchen of the Hermann–Grima House, a structure whose architecture and grounds reflect the elegance of New Orleans during its Golden Age, 1830–1860.

Fireplace cooking can be observed on the first and third Thursdays of each month, October through April. Baking in a large brick bake oven, and cooking on a special tile cooking counter with stew-holes, are also demonstrated.

A Creole cookery book, published by the restoration, is available.

Maryland

THE NATIONAL COLONIAL FARM OF THE ACCOKEEK FOUNDATION, Route 1, Box 697, Accokeek, Maryland 20607. Telephone: (301) 283-2113.

The re-creation of an eighteenth-century middle-class tobacco plantation is the setting for fireplace cooking and beehive oven baking. Cooking demonstrations are held daily during the summer months, at which time visitors can observe a typical simple noon meal being prepared.

Massachusetts

HANCOCK SHAKER VILLAGE, Intersection of Routes 20 and 41, Pittsfield, Massachusetts. (Mailing address: Shaker Community, Inc., P.O. Box 898, Pittsfield, Massachusetts 01201.) Telephone: (413) 443-0188.

Hancock Shaker Village is a nineteenth-century restored village depicting Shaker farm life and crafts housed in twenty historic buildings on a thousand-acre site.

While there is no open-hearth cooking at this restoration, beehive oven baking can be observed on Saturdays from June 1 through October 31.

Workshops held in the summer months frequently include instruction in firing and baking in the beehive oven. A schedule noting the dates of these events is available from the village.

HARLOW OLD FORT HOUSE, 119 Sandwich Street, Plymouth, Massachusetts 02360. Telephone: (617) 746-3017.

The Harlow Old Fort House is a seventeenth-century gambrel-roof dwelling built in 1677 by Major William Harlow, a second generation Mayflower descendant. Fireplace cooking is performed here five or six times during the summer, weather permitting, and always on Thanksgiving Day. Only antique implements are used to execute recipes, which are from Plymouth Colony cookbooks that are published by the restoration. The books are for sale.

OLD STURBRIDGE VILLAGE, Route 20, Sturbridge, Massachusetts 01566. Telephone: (617) 347-3362.

Perhaps the best known living history museum in the Northeast, Old Sturbridge Village portrays family, work, and community life in nineteenth-century rural New England. As befits a restoration of its stature, an abundance of activities relating to open-hearth cooking are performed here.

Fireplace cooking can be observed daily in at least two of the village's households. Every morning in the Freeman farmhouse, preparations for the noon meal are in progress. Twice a week its beehive oven is fired for breads, pies, and other baked foods. While daily at the Fitch household, a center village dwelling, cooking for the evening meal or afternoon tea is underway.

Other homes in the Village that demonstrate fireplace cooking, though less frequently, are the Salem Town house and Richardson house.

Instruction in fireplace cooking is offered in the restoration's Crafts at Close Range program. These classes include one-hour "experiences" for visiting school children and six-hour cooking sessions for adults. Class sizes, times, and techniques vary. For further information, write: Secretary of Special Events, Old Sturbridge Village.

PLIMOTH PLANTATION, Warren Avenue, Plymouth, Massachusetts. (Mailing address: Box 1620, Plymouth, Massachusetts 02360.) Telephone: (617) 746-1622.

Community life in the famous 1627 Pilgrim settlement is re-created through a living history format at Plimoth Plantation. The "Pilgrims" in the village take their roles and the living history presentation very seriously. A response to the question, How long have you worked here? elicited the response, "Oh, for about seven years . . . ever since the Mayflower landed in 1620."

Fireplace cooking is performed in all of the settlement's authentically primitive dwellings, as part of the housewives' daily routine. The simplest one-pot meals, referred to as pottage, are prepared, reflecting the period and way of life of the settlers' existence. Only the most basic cooking implements are in evidence. An outdoor communal bake oven is on display and is infrequently fired.

Michigan

GREENFIELD VILLAGE AND HENRY FORD MUSEUM, Dearborn, Michigan 48121. Telephone: (313) 271-1620.

November's Cooking Weekends at Greenfield Village afford visitors a special glimpse of America's culinary past. In four of the village's historic homes (two of which rely on fireplaces for cooking) techniques and foods appropriate to the age and origin of the dwellings are presented. The cooking implements used, the table settings, the recipes, in short, everything, even "the aroma in the air of the herbs and spices," is designed to be true to the period of the house.

For example, in the Susquehanna House, a 1700's plantation home, reflector oven roasting of a turkey is shown. While at Plymouth House, a duck on a spit and a fish are roasted in the tradition of mid-1600's cookery.

Other Special Event weekends throughout the year often include open-hearth cooking. Especially elaborate are the cooking and baking preparations for the Christmas celebration in the village.

A number of interesting and informative courses for adults and teenagers on fireplace cooking technique and early American foods are offered by the Edison Institute, whose extensive education program is described in the Village literature as "an extension and intensification of the collections and activities of Greenfield Village and the Henry Ford Museum."

Food- and cooking-related courses and workshops offered by the Institute in the past have been: Colonial Fireplace Cooking; Cooking With Herbs; Domestic Activities, A Woman's World; and Early American Recipes.

HISTORIC MACKINAC ISLAND, Mackinac City, Mackinac Island, Michigan. (Mailing Address: Mackinac Island Park Commission, P.O. Box 370, Mackinac Island, Michigan 49757.) Telephone: (906) 847-3328.

On Mackinac Island numerous and varied fireplace cooking traditions can be observed at historic Fort Michilimackinac and in the nearby Indian Dormitory.

The kitchens of the Priest's House and the Picquet House, located inside Fort Michilimackinac, demonstrate fireplace cooking every day during the summer months. The Piquet House is a reconstructed British home and, as such, emphasizes British culinary tastes and habits. The Priest's house prepares mostly French dishes.

American fireplace cooking is also demonstrated daily in the 1840 kitchen of the Indian Dormitory, located just outside the fort. A wide range of open-hearth cooking techniques can be observed in its well-equipped kitchen. The food prepared here reflects research from original cookbooks of the period, and incorporates regional specialties and ingredients, as well.

Minnesota

HISTORIC FORT SNELLING, Fort Snelling Exits, Minnesota, Highways 5 or 55. (Mailing address: c/o Building 25, Fort Snelling, Minnesota 55111.) Telephone: (612) 726-1171.

The sixteen buildings, fourteen of which are stone, and 1,500 feet of stone wall, all built by Colonel Snelling's troops in only four years, constitute the bulk of Fort Snelling, an army fortification erected between 1820–1825 and interpreted to the year 1827.

Fireplace cooking is demonstrated in many of the fort's fireplaces. On a daily basis, one or more of the following kinds of cooking may be observed: army mess preparation for a squad of twelve; cooking and/or baking for an enlisted man's family; baking of army ration bread in the bakeshop; and preparation of specialty items in the Colonel's kitchen.

Missouri

MISSOURI TOWN 1855, Lake Jacomo, Rt. 1, Box 124, Blue Springs, Missouri 64015. Telephone: (816) 795-8200.

A Missouri frontier town as it existed more than a century ago is the focus of this living history museum.

Visitors can observe fireplace cooking at random times in the kitchen of Withers House and the tap-room of the Chevis–Samuel Tavern. Open-hearth cooking is also a regular feature of the restoration's annual Fall Festival of Crafts, Art, and Music.

Each spring the Chevis–Samuel Tavern is the setting for the fireplace cooking segment of the University of Missouri, Kansas City college-accredited course: Social History of Missouri, 1840's–1860's.

WORNALL HOUSE, 61st Terrace and Wornall Road, Kansas City, Missouri 64113. Telephone: (816) 444-1858.

The Wornall House is an 1858 farm home characteristic of the life of Southern farmers who migrated to western Missouri in the mid-nineteenth century.

Fireplace cooking can generally be observed here on Wednesdays from October through May. The demonstrations, given by docents dressed in period costume, cover a discussion of foods grown, methods of food preservation and preparation, and typical menus, as well as fireplace cooking executed with antique implements.

We suggest you check with the restoration before you plan a visit, since in some months the Wednesday demonstrations are reserved for school groups only.

New Jersey

THE ISRAEL CRANE HOUSE, 110 Orange Avenue, Montclair, New Jersey. (Mailing address: Montclair Historical Society, Box 322, Montclair, New Jersey 07042.) Telephone: (201) 744-1796.

A wealth of information on open-hearth cooking is offered by the Montclair Historical Society at their restored and relocated Israel Crane House, which dates back to the eighteenth-century.

On Sunday afternoons during winter months, when the house is open to the public, visitors can observe a variety of fireplace cooking techniques being performed in the well-equipped kitchen of the house. These techniques include the use of the tin kitchen, Dutch oven, and beehive oven.

Other days of the week, cooking demonstrations for school groups can be arranged. On these occasions, the visiting children are invited to taste the fireplace fare prepared and to stir the soup, or try their hand at other simple kitchen tasks.

A series of open-hearth cooking classes for adults (a maximum of fifteen participants), in which complete meals based on period menus are prepared and then eaten, have been scheduled in the past on Tuesday mornings. Mini- or one-day seminars on fireplace cooking have also been offered.

A great deal of research by members of the Montclair Historical Society went into the reconstruction of the Crane House kitchen, and this effort is reflected in the depth and accuracy of the information presented in the cooking classes, as well as in the demonstrations. This research also produced two excellent and well-known cookbooks, both of which can be ordered from the restoration. They are: *Fanny Pierson Crane, Her Receipts, 1796*, a paperback; and a more ambitious volume published in hardcover by Holt, Rinehart & Winston in connection with the celebration of the Nation's bicentennial, *The Thirteen Colonies Cookbook*.

MILLER CORY MUSEUM, 614 Mountain Avenue, Westfield, New Jersey. (Mailing address: P.O. Box 455, Westfield, New Jersey 07091.) Telephone: (201) 232-1776.

A living history museum that depicts life on an eighteenth-century farm in the West Fields of Elizabeth.

Fireplace cooking can be observed here in the Frazie Building every Sunday in September, October, November, December, March, April, May, and June. These demonstrations feature the preparation of a complete meal appropriate to the season. Reproductions of antique implements are used for cooking purposes.

A paperback cookbook, *The Groaning Board, A Collection of 18th Century Receipts*, is available from the restoration.

New York

THE FARMERS' MUSEUM INC., Cooperstown, New York 13326. Telephone: (607) 547-2593.

Spanning 1800–1860, the Farmers' Museum includes a barn, an exhibition building, and a recreated village crossroads consisting of fourteen period structures moved to their present location from within a hundred-mile radius of Cooperstown.

The 1797 Lippitt house kitchen is the setting for daily fireplace cooking demonstrations, where baking in either a beehive oven or Dutch oven can be observed.

Instruction in fireplace cooking is offered to elementary and junior high school students as part of the museum's winter workshop program.

FORT CRAILO STATE HISTORIC SITE, 9 1/2 Riverside Avenue, Rensselaer, New York 12144. Telephone: (518) 463-8738.

Fort Crailo, built in the first decade of the eighteenth century by Hendrick Van Rensselaer, is now a museum interpreting the history of the Colonial Dutch culture of the Hudson Valley.

Fireplace cooking for groups (a maximum of twenty-five) can be arranged by advance request. In these workshop/demonstrations participants prepare a complete meal and sample the finished product.

GENESEE COUNTRY VILLAGE, Flint Hill Road, Mumford, New York. (Mailing address: P.O. Box 1819, Rochester, New York 14603.) Telephone: (716) 538-6822.

A village of over fifty buildings depicts a typical Genesee Valley settlement from the late eighteenth through the nineteenth centuries. Daily demonstrations of fireplace cooking of various levels of sophistication can be observed here. In the Log House, c. 1795, only cornmeal-based foods are prepared. In the Farmhouse, c. 1820, demonstrations of butter and cheese making and other simple cooking are performed. The most elaborate fireplace cooking techniques can be observed in the Greek Revival Manor house, c. 1820, a household which employed a servant who did the cooking.

KNOX HEADQUARTERS STATE HISTORIC SITE, Vails Gate, New York. (Mailing address: P.O. Box 207, Vails Gate, New York 12584.) Telephone: (914) 561-5498.

Built in the Georgian style by Thomas Ellison in 1754, this stone house was occupied at various times during the Revolutionary campaigns by important American military officers, the most famous of whom was General Henry Knox.

The restoration, now a state historic site, contains two furnished cooking hearths, one of which will be used for demonstration purposes. The fireplace cooking demonstrations are still in the researching and planning stages, and will be geared in particular to school-aged children. Check with the restoration for a current progress report on these activities.

MUSEUM VILLAGE IN ORANGE COUNTY, Monroe, New York 10950. Telephone (914) 782-8247.

Fireplace cooking and beehive oven baking are featured during Museum Village's Fall Festival, held in October. The village, consisting of forty buildings, portrays nineteenth-century life through the tools and other objects in its collections.

Winter workshops offering instruction in fireplace cooking and baking, as well as other early American crafts, are usually scheduled from the beginning of October through the second week in December.

OBADIAH SMITH HOUSE, 853 Johnland Road, Kings Park, Long Island, New York. (Mailing address: Smithtown Historical Society, P.O. Box 69, Smithtown, New York 11787.) Telephone: (516) 265-6768.

Open-hearth cooking demonstrations for children are held on an infrequent and pre-arranged basis at the Obadiah Smith House, c. 1710. On these occasions, simple recipes, such as spider corn bread, are executed to allow the children to participate in the preparation of the food. The kitchen's original brick bake oven still exists and is occasionally fired.

The Smithtown Historical Society has plans to expand the fireplace cooking activities at the restoration as funds for training more docents in this specialty become available.

OLD BETHPAGE VILLAGE RESTORATION, Round Swamp Road, Old Bethpage, Long Island, New York 11804. Telephone: (516) 420-5280.

A full complement of cooking techniques, from broiling to beehive oven baking, are demonstrated daily in the fireplace kitchens of Old Bethpage Village, a recreated rural village depicting life and work styles on Long Island in the eighteenth and nineteenth centuries. Around Thanksgiving and over Labor Day weekend, the preparation of more elaborate meals can be observed.

On request, cooking workshops can occasionally be arranged.

RICHMONDTOWN RESTORATION, 441 Clarke Avenue, Staten Island, New York 10306. Telephone: (212) 351-1611.

Described in its brochure as "a restoration in progress," Richmondtown traces in its exhibits the evolution of an American village from the seventeenth through the twentieth centuries.

Fireplace cooking and beehive oven baking are demonstrated on Old Home Day (usually the third Sunday in October), and on Tuesdays and Thursdays in July and August.

Open-hearth cooking classes, limited to six participants, are scheduled to begin in the Spring of 1980.

SLEEPY HOLLOW RESTORATIONS, 150 White Plains Road, Tarrytown, New York 10591. Telephone: (914) 631-8200.

The three estates that make up the Sleepy Hollow Restorations—Van Cortlandt Manor, Phillipsburg Manor, and Sunnyside—all feature fireplace cooking as a daily attraction to their visitors.

In addition to these daily demonstrations, a variety of intensive cooking workshops are offered by the restoration. General workshops in fireplace cooking for adults and children are held in January, February, and March. All participants (four to six each day) prepare a full meal and then enjoy eating it together.

Other more specialized food-related workshops that have been given in the past covered beehive oven baking, woodstove cookery, food preservation, cheese-making, and butchering and smoking meat.

The information on open-hearth cooking presented at the Sleepy Hollow restorations is based on unpublished eighteenth-century manuscripts that have been handed down in the families who have owned these homes.

WILLIAM SIDNEY MOUNT HOMESTEAD, The Museums at Stony Brook, Stony Brook, New York 11790. Telephone: (516) 751-0066.

Open-hearth cooking is a special attraction of seasonal house tours held during the month of December at the William Sidney Mount Homestead. Originally built in the eighteenth century, the dwelling was enlarged in the nineteenth and again in the twentieth centuries. Previously the residence of two noted American artists, it was designated as a National Historic Landmark in 1965.

The fireplace cooking performed for these tours usually involves the use of the Dutch oven, as well as other basic hearth cooking implements. A brick bake oven, while not utilized for these demonstrations, completes the kitchen fireplace setting.

North Carolina

OLD SALEM, INC., Drawer F, Salem Station, Winston-Salem, North Carolina 27108. Telephone: (919) 723-3688.

During the summer months, fireplace cooking is frequently demonstrated at Old Salem, Inc., a restored Moravian congregation town of the period 1766-1856.

Museum classes in fireplace cooking are offered, and special programs for student groups can be arranged.

TRYON PALACE, 608 Pollock St., New Bern, North Carolina. (Mailing Address: Box 1007, New Bern, North Carolina 28560.) Telephone: (919) 638-5109.

The kitchen of Tryon Palace is in a separate building—the East Wing—as one would expect in an elegant Southern mansion that served as the capital and governor's residence of the Royal Colony of North Carolina and later as its first state capital.

Fireplace cooking can be observed from November through February. These demonstrations are primarily designed for school groups as part of a Colonial Living Tour. Both English and American antique cooking utensils have been used to furnish the kitchen.

Ohio

HALE FARM AND VILLAGE, 2686 Oak Hill Road, Bath, Ohio. (Mailing address: Box 256, Bath, Ohio 44210.) Telephone: (216) 666-3711.

Cooking in the fireplace or baking in the brick bake oven can be observed on the weekends at Hale Farm and Village, a living history museum portraying the life of nineteenth-century settlers of the Western Reserve.

On exhibit at the restoration are two cooking fireplaces. One is in the 1835 salt box; the other in the 1826 Hale House. Hearth-baked johnnycake spread with freshly churned butter is offered to visitors.

Instruction in fireplace cooking has been included in a course conducted at the site by Cleveland Community College entitled, A Day in the 19th Century.

JOHNSTON FARM, Piqua Historical Area, 9845 N. Hardin Road, Piqua, Ohio 45356. Telephone: (513) 773-2522.

The 174-acre Piqua Historical Area includes among its many interesting attractions the restored 1810–1815 farm and home of John Johnston, Ohio Indian Agent. Here, fireplace cooking with antique implements can be observed daily.

Cooking demonstrations in the past have featured entire meals based on period menus, but are now limited almost exclusively to baking, which is accomplished either with a Dutch oven in the fireplace or in the adjacent brick bake oven. (The baking technique utilized depends on the personnel available.) Samples of the baked foods are given to the visitors.

While no classes in fireplace cooking are scheduled, the restoration's interpreters are happy to talk about fireplace cooking techniques, and seem willing to set up a teaching session for anyone expressing special interest.

Pennsylvania

THE ALEXANDER SCHAEFFER FARM MUSEUM, Historic Schaefferstown, Schaefferstown, Pennsylvania 17088. Telephone: (717) 949-2244.

Fireplace cooking can be observed daily at Historic Schaefferstown, a living history museum portraying eighteenth- and nineteenth-century farm life of the German settlers of Pennsylvania, commonly known as the Pennsylvania Dutch.

Traditional Pennsylvania Dutch fare is prepared in the fireplace here and baking is performed in an old "squirrel tail" oven on Wednesdays and Saturdays. Visitors are invited to participate in the firing and use of the bake oven.

In August a class in Pennsylvania Dutch cooking is usually held. In these sessions, one-pot meals, soups, the use of the Dutch oven, spider, and other ethnic foods and techniques are covered.

Annual festivals, July's Folklore Festival and September's Harvest Fair, include among their extensive activities and demonstrations firing of the bake oven, bread-making, cake-baking, and fruit and vegetable drying, along with "some sort of Pennsylvania Dutch food (served) at every turn," to quote the Schaefferstown brochure.

COLONIAL PENNSYLVANIA PLANTATION, Ridley Creek State Park, Edgemont, Pennsylvania. (Mailing address: Box 150, Edgemont, Pennsylvania 19028.) Telephone: (215) 353-1777.

Colonial Pennsylvania Plantation is a working farm typical of those found in southeastern Pennsylvania in the 1770's. Fireplace cooking can be observed on Saturdays and Sundays, and beehive oven baking is performed infrequently when firewood is plentiful.

Only foods commonly eaten in the eighteenth century are prepared, using authentic recipes and cooking techniques. Workshop/demonstrations in fireplace cooking can be arranged for school groups upon request.

HISTORIC FALLSINGTON, 4 Yardly Avenue, Fallsington, Pennsylvania 19054. Telephone: (215) 295-6567.

Fireplace cooking is demonstrated here on Fallsington Day, regularly celebrated on the second Saturday in October in this pre-Revolutionary village where William Penn worshipped. While the cooking is only a once-a-year event, we've included it because the meal prepared at the hearth of the 1685 Moon-Williamson Log Cabin is raffled off and served at the end of the day to the lucky winners.

HOPEWELL VILLAGE NATIONAL HISTORIC SITE, R.D. #1, Box 345, Elverson, Pennsylvania 19520. Telephone: (215) 582-8773.

Open-hearth cooking, including firing of bake ovens, can be observed every day from June through August at Hopewell Village, a restored iron-producing community that thrived in the eighteenth and nineteenth centuries. Recipes and cooking techniques reflect the period 1820–1840 and utilize many vegetables and herbs grown on the site. Reproduction cooking implements and utensils are used in these demonstrations.

PENNSBURY MANOR, Rural Route 9, Morrisville, Pennsylvania 19067. Telephone: (215) 946-0400.

Fireplace cooking is currently demonstrated only three or four times a year at Pennsbury, William Penn's beautiful estate, which overlooks the Delaware River just outside of Historic Fallsington.

In the planning stages, though, is a more ambitious program of cooking activities which will utilize the site's three cooking fireplaces and its two bake ovens on a more regular basis. Reproductions of antique cooking implements and utensils will be used to furnish these hearths. Meals and recipes prepared will be from Gulielna Penn's (William Penn's wife) personal collection. Produce grown in the manor's gardens will be used whenever possible for cooking.

PENNSYLVANIA FARM MUSEUM OF LANDIS VALLEY, 2451 Kissel Hill Road, Lancaster, Pennsylvania 17601. Telephone: (717) 569-0401.

Fireplace cooking demonstrations occur most days (except Sundays) at the Pennsylvania Farm Museum of Landis Valley, a restoration interpreting the history of rural Pennsylvania life of the eighteenth and nineteenth centuries. Antique implements are used, for the most part, at the cooking hearth.

Other food-related activities feature the preservation of the produce of the farm: drying its garden vegetables, smoking the meat of the slaughtered livestock, and grinding the corn grown into cornmeal.

Instruction in fireplace cooking and baking is offered to small groups (usually less than twelve).

QUIET VALLEY LIVING HISTORICAL FARM, R.D. #2, Box 2495, Stroudsburg, Pennsylvania 18360. Telephone: (717) 992-6161.

A large cellar/kitchen fireplace is the setting for daily open-hearth cooking demonstrations at Quiet Valley, a farm and museum which spans the eighteenth and nineteenth centuries. These demonstrations include the use of the Dutch oven, griddle, swivel toaster, and kettles of various sizes.

An authentically restored brick bake oven is also fired regularly on Saturdays during the summer, and on other special occasions, as well. At these times, large quantitites of bread, pies, casseroles, and roasts are some of the foods baked in the oven.

Fireplace cooking is presently taught only to the staff of the farm, but infrequent workshops on the topic have been offered to the restoration's membership. The annual Harvest Festival, held each year on Columbus Day Weekend, features a wide variety of Colonial foods.

1696 THOMAS MASSEY HOUSE, Lawrence Road at Springhouse Road, Broomall, Pennsylvania. (Mailing address: P.O. Box 18, Broomall, Pennsylvania 19008.) Telephone: (215) 353-3644.

Open-hearth cooking and beehive oven baking can be observed during the summer months at the Thomas Massey House, dated 1696. At other times of the year cooking demonstrations are held by special arrangement with the museum's curator, who also happens to be its open-hearth cooking specialist. Both antique and reproduction implements are used at the hearth.

A unique feature of the restoration are the Colonial fireplace dinners the staff will prepare for private groups of up to twenty persons. These dinners are a way of raising funds for the house, and include only foods prepared in the fireplace.

Rhode Island

COGGESHALL FARM MUSEUM, Colt State Park, Route 114, Bristol, Rhode Island 02809. Telephone: (401) 253-9062.

Coggeshall is a restoration of an eighteenth-century working farm that includes organic vegetable gardens, herb gardens, Colonial orchards, farm animals, in addition to the traditional and more usual craft demonstrations.

Open-hearth cooking can be observed here on Saturday and Sunday afternoons from July 4th through Labor Day. Special programs, including both open-hearth cooking demonstrations and classes, are offered for school groups.

WANTON–LYMAN–HAZARD HOUSE, 17 Broadway, Newport, Rhode Island 02840. Telephone: (401) 846-0813.

Fireplace cooking using antique implements is demonstrated every day during the summer months when the Wanton–Lyman–Hazard House is open. Built c. 1690 in the Jacobean style, the house is dominated by one central, massive chimney with outlets in all of its rooms. It is the earliest restored Colonial home in Newport.

Samples of food prepared are offered to visitors. And, if you especially like what you taste, a cookbook, collecting these recipes and those of other Newport and Rhode Island Colonial specialties, can be purchased.

Utah

MARY FIELDING SMITH HOUSE, Pioneer Trail State Park, 2601 Sunnyside Avenue, Salt Lake City, Utah 84108. Telephone: (801) 533-5881.

The Mary Fielding Smith House, a one-room adobe cottage, will be the setting for fireplace cooking in this outdoor museum and pioneer village typical of the period before 1869 in Pioneer Utah.

The restoration is currently researching fireplace cooking in its region and plans to demonstrate it on an irregular basis from May through October.

Virginia

THE COLONIAL WILLIAMSBURG FOUNDATION, Post Office Box 627, Williamsburg, Virginia 23185. Telephone: (804) 229-1000.

Fireplace cooking at Colonial Williamsburg, perhaps the most famous, most elegant, and most visited restoration in the United States, is performed daily in the kitchen of the Wythe House, located in the historic area. To complement these demonstrations, authentic Colonial Virginia fare, such as peanut soup and spoon bread, can be sampled by visitors at the restoration's three period taverns. In addition, a number of excellent cookbooks covering these same foods and recipes are sold in its gift shops.

A separate and very special program covering fireplace cooking, expressly designed and reserved for school groups, is offered at Colonial Williamsburg's Powell–Waller House. In the past this program has presented fireplace cooking demonstrations to approximately 75,000 students a year!

Recently the Powell–Waller House kitchen has been equipped with a full complement of fireplace cooking implements, and a staff of twenty is being trained to demonstrate and instruct students in the open-hearth cooking process. Plans are to demonstrate fireplace cooking techniques to student groups of twenty to twenty-five, and to involve groups of ten to twelve in cooking workshops that will take up the better part of a day. The latter workshops will only be held during Williamsburg's less busy tourist season, the winter. The open-hearth cooking techniques both demonstrated and taught at Williamsburg will run the gamut from simple one-pot dinners to meals with several courses involving roasting, baking, etc. Antique implements as well as reproductions will be used.

Teachers are requested to make scheduling arrangements for their students with the Powell–Waller House Educational Programmers.

GEORGE WASHINGTON BIRTHPLACE NATIONAL MONUMENT, Washington's Birthplace, Virginia 22575. Telephone: (804) 224-0196.

A fire is lit every day in the cooking hearth of the farmhouse where George Washington was born. Now a living history museum, the re-created tobacco farm portrays the early years of George Washington's life.

Meals based on Colonial recipes are frequently prepared in the kitchen fireplace, although, to quote the staff, "not on a daily basis because of other pressing chores that need to be done on the farm."

TURKEY RUN FARM, Geroge Washington Memorial Parkway, McLean, Virginia 22101. Telephone: (703) 557-1356.

Fireplace cooking at Turkey Run Farm is demonstrated as a part of the daily meal preparation in the farm cabin, and is best observed between 10:00 A.M. and 1:00 P.M.

Reproductions of eighteenth-century cooking implements are used, and menus are based on information from British and American cookbooks, diaries, and travel journals of the period. These resources, combined with the limitations of seasonal foodstuffs and the economic level of a low-income tobacco planter in the 1770's, determine the diet and thus the foods cooked in the fireplace.

Farm visitors are encouraged to observe and ask questions about the cooking procedures, which include spit roasting, baking, frying, stewing, boiling, etc. In addition to cooking techniques, all levels of eighteenth-century food preparation and preservation are practiced, including drying, pickling, salting, butchering, and curing.

Wyoming

FORT LARAMIE NATIONAL HISTORIC SITE, Fort Laramie, Wyoming 82212. Telephone: (307) 837-2221.

Although fireplace cooking is not demonstrated at Fort Laramie, visitors can observe traditional "army bread" being mixed, kneaded, and then baked in the fort's reproduction brick ovens. The original 1803 post bread recipe is followed to produce the loaves, and the baking process is a daily attraction during the summer months.

10

Sources for Equipping Your Cooking Hearth

ireplace cooking implements, as you have probably noticed, are not sold in the housewares sections of your local department or hardware stores. They are a little too exotic for these outlets. Nonetheless, they are readily available. In this chapter, we have included a list of some of the better-known sources for these implements. Included are three categories of source: retail outlets and mail-order sources for ready-made items; working craftsmen—blacksmiths and tinsmiths who are employed or recommended by restorations; and references to articles on how to make implements yourself. Between them, you should be able to fully equip your fireplace kitchen according to the dictates of your budget, taste, and skill.

The retail outlet and mail-order section covers suppliers of reasonably priced, mass-produced or machine-made, but still very serviceable, items. They are a good place to begin your shopping. Most of these outlets, the Boy Scouts of America, for example, will probably have the implement desired in stock. So, if you're especially eager to get started, this is one way that you can satisfy an urge to begin cooking immediately, or at least as soon as the mail reaches your door.

If you can't find what you want in the ready-made section, the blacksmiths and tinsmiths we have listed will produce almost any implement to order. Their work is usually expensive, but the results are of a high grade, often museum quality, and are aesthetically pleasing. In general, the work of these craftsmen merits the extra expense. One drawback to dealing with craftsmen is that getting an item through one of them is often a somewhat slower process than ordering the same item ready-made. Many craftsmen produce on demand only. Depending on what you have requested, and on the craftsman's backlog of orders, this can mean a delay of weeks. This is not the option to choose if you need your implement in a hurry.

The articles on making your own hearth cooking implements may present an alternative for the talented few. But iron-working and tinsmithing are very specialized crafts, and are perhaps best left to the trained artisan; at least, they should be tackled under his supervision. This can be done in one of the many adult or extension courses on these topics that are currently gaining popularity.

Equipping Your Fireplace With Antiques

Equipping your fireplace with antique cooking implements is by far the most expensive option for the fireplace cook, and is a pursuit unto itself. But, since some may want to consider this possibility—and since we are collectors ourselves—we felt it appropriate to give some observations on buying and using antiques for cooking before turning to more practical sources.

Antique dealers who specialize in early American kitchen equipment are a logical place to begin your search, but dealers who limit their stock exclusively to these items are few and far between. Most combine cooking pots and implements with other tools, such as those used for woodworking, blacksmithing, and tinsmithing. The largest of these dealers in the U.S. is Iron Horse Antiques Inc., in Poultney, Vermont, though most any dealer who favors early American primitives is likely to have an antique iron or tin cooking implement or two in his inventory. Don't be shocked by the prices! Rare examples of early American kitchen implements—a teakettle with a tilter, or spit andirons, for example—have been bid up to the $300 price range at recent auctions, supposedly a wholesale source. When early pieces are signed by their makers they command even higher prices. Good places to look for older, if not yet antique, implements at more reasonable prices are flea markets and even garage or tag sales. These sources can harbor real finds for the knowledgeable and lucky buyer.

Equipping your fireplace solely with antiques may turn out to be an unrealistically drawn-out and unpredictable process. Antiques are one of a kind, and, since a dealer's stock varies from month to month, the exact pot, trammel, or other accessory you are after may not be available precisely when you need it—or ever, for that matter, at a price you are willing to pay.

When buying antiques to use for actual cooking, you must be sure that they are in good condition or that it is possible to have them cleaned and restored to working order. Frequently, antique metal pots are painted or encrusted with rust, which must be removed before they can be used for preparing food. This can be done quite easily by professional metal strippers who use strong chemicals or sandblasting to clean the surfaces. But be wary of pieces that may be worn too thin or are too rusted to withstand the rigors of these methods. Also, avoid pots that have been converted to planters and have drainage holes drilled in their bottoms, and kettles with cracked or badly chipped enamel linings. These flaws cannot be mended. In general, though, most wrought iron and tin pieces can be repaired by a skilled blacksmith or tinsmith. Broken cast iron pieces are a little more difficult to fix, but we have had some success replacing broken-off feet on these implements, as well.

Antique implements must also be handled with great care. Age and repeated exposure to the extreme temperatures of the fire have rendered their metals very brittle. Cracks appear, and small pieces snap off with the slightest provocation. A broken kettle foot, a cracked toaster, and a lost tin kitchen spout were just a few of the casualties our collections sustained while testing the recipes for this book.

Repairs are possible, as we just mentioned, but we are obligated to add that they do diminish the value of an antique object. And, while we love handling old pieces and cooking with them, we concede that they are perhaps best left to enhance the setting of your hearth. In fact, most restorations use only fine reproductions of antique cooking implements, made to their specifications or copied from originals in their collections, for fireplace cooking, a practice that preserves their true antiques for the enjoyment and education of future generations.

Retail Outlets and Mail-Order Sources for Ready-Made Items

Here are a few selected outlets we have discovered for fireplace cooking implements. Their diversity and specialties should give you some ideas about stores in your area that are likely to stock these same items. Camping suppliers are a good bet for camp Dutch ovens, while sophisticated gourmet cooking and housewares stores usually stock fish grills. At a Pottery Barn outlet in New Jersey (part of a national chain), for example, we bought a fish grill, a gridiron (it was labeled a French grill), and a wire basket corn-popper. All were very reasonably priced. Also, don't overlook the fireplace stores that are cropping up everywhere, as they always carry corn-poppers, fireplace pokers, shovels, tongs, and bellows, or have catalogs from which one can order these items.

THE BOY SCOUTS OF AMERICA, Supply Division, P.O. Box 61030, Dallas-Fort Worth Airport, Texas 75261.
Cast iron camp Dutch oven.

THE BRIDGE KITCHENWARE CORPORATION, 214 East 52nd Street, New York, New York 10022.
Fish grills (numerous shapes and sizes stocked. Claims to have the largest selection anywhere).

BROOKSTONE, 5 Vose Farm Road, Peterborough, New Hampshire 03458.
A crème brûlée iron which can be used as a salamander for browning off the tops of other foods, as well as for caramelizing the top of this dessert.

ENERGY HARVESTER STORE, Box 19K, Fitzwilliam, New Hampshire 03447.
3 1/2 qt. cast iron kettle with handle.

GARDEN WAY CATALOG, Charlotte, Vermont 05445.

9 qt. cast iron camp Dutch oven, 6 qt. cast iron teakettle.

GENERAL HOUSEWARES CORPORATION, P.O. Box 4066, Terre Haute, Indiana 47804.

5 qt. hanging bean pot, 9 qt. cast iron camp Dutch oven.

IRON CRAFT INC., 1 Pleasant Street, Freedom, New Hampshire 03836.

A variety of hard-to-find, cast iron pots and other implements, including reproductions of the gypsy kettle (5 qt. and 2 3/4 gal. size), fireplace cranes, corn-poppers, basket grills, bellows, iron beehive oven doors, camp Dutch ovens in four sizes, etc. Write for their extensive catalog on cast iron cookware and accessories.

LEMEE'S FIREPLACE EQUIPMENT, 815 Bedford Street, Bridgewater, Massachusetts 02324.

Fireplace cranes, tools, and cast iron pots.

LONG ASSOCIATES, 222 Friend Street, Boston, Massachusetts 02114.

Fireplace cranes.

LODGE MANUFACTURING CO., South Pittsburg, Tennessee 37380.

Cast iron camp Dutch ovens, in even sizes 8–14.

MINUTEMAN INTERNATIONAL CO. LTD., 8 Nickerson Road, Lexington, Massachusetts 02173.

Cast iron teakettles.

OLD GUILFORD FORGE, On the Green, Guilford, Connecticut 06437.

Fireplace cranes, gypsy kettles, S hooks, an adjustable trammel, numerous fireplace tools, and even a low pine stool with a rush seat for comfortable cooking at the hearth!

PAINE AND CHRISCOT, INC., 1187 Second Avenue, New York, New York 10021.

Fireplace cranes.

SIMS STOVES, Lovell, Wyoming 82431.

Reflector bake ovens (the only source we know of for this item).

STURBRIDGE YANKEE WORKSHOP, Brimfield Turnpike, Sturbridge, Massachusetts 01566.

Fireplace cranes, hearth trivet, corn-poppers, and fireplace tools.

WILLIAMS–SONOMA, Mail Order Department, P.O. Box 3792, San Francisco, California 94119.

A round cast iron muffin pan which fits into a Dutch oven, an Italian pizzelle or wafer iron, a Belgian waffle iron, and English baking (crumpet) rings.

Made to Order: Working Blacksmiths and Tinsmiths

Below is a list, by state, of restorations that employ blacksmiths or tinsmiths to demonstrate their crafts. In the process of demonstrating, these craftsmen usually make quantities of the simpler fireplace cooking accessories (S hooks, for example) which are then sold in the site's gift shop. But most have the skills to make the more elaborate cooking implements—tin kitchens, spit andirons, etc.—and will do so on special order.

Quite a few of the restorations surveyed didn't have the facilities or finances to employ a blacksmith or tinsmith on a regular basis. They did, though, refer us to a number of excellent local craftsmen whom they had either engaged on occasion to demonstrate their crafts, or from whom they had commissioned reproductions of cooking implements to equip their museum hearths. Hence, interspersed with the restorations in our list, are these recommended independent tinsmiths and blacksmiths. These artisans are usually masters at their craft and work at it full-time. They will make most items to order only, but can make most any implement within their specialty. Some have brochures and price lists. Others operate on a more informal basis, but will send photographs of their work and estimates upon request.

Keep in mind that all of these craftsmen, restoration-affiliated or not, will usually do repair work, as well.

Arizona

PIONEER ARIZONA LIVING HISTORY MUSEUM, P.O. Box 11242, Phoenix, Arizona 85061.

John Cochran, the resident blacksmith, will make many items to order, as will their tinsmith, Charles Hartwell.

Kent Gugler (blacksmith), 1562 Shoup Street, Prescott, Arizona 86301.

Trivets, forks, fire tools.

Florida

SAN AGUSTIN ANTIGUO, Historic St. Augustine Preservation Board, P.O. Box 1987, St. Augustine, Florida 32084.

Alvin Mickler, the restoration's blacksmith, makes andirons, trammels, S hooks, and other iron implements to order.

Georgia

GEORGIA AGRIRAMA, P.O. Box Q, Tifton, Georgia 31794.

Dennis Snyder, their blacksmith, can make most equipment needed for open-hearth cooking, from S hooks to andirons. Most items are custom made and prices are quoted by the order.

THE TULLIE SMITH HOUSE, 3099 Andrews Drive, N.W., Atlanta, Georgia 30305.

The craft shop carries trivets, andirons, trammels, and S hooks, and will take orders for any wrought iron pot or utensil.

R. Darryl Herren (blacksmith), Olive Forge, Rt. 6, Box 92, Milledgeville, Georgia 31061.

Trivets, toasters, toasting forks, andirons, etc. Brochure available.

Indiana

CONNOR PRAIRIE PIONEER SETTLEMENT, 30 Conner Lane, Noblesville, Indiana 46060.

John Hollis, their working blacksmith, will make reproductions of any period implement to order.

Iowa

LIVING HISTORY FARMS, Rural Rt. #1, Des Moines, Iowa 50322.

Marty Hildreth, their blacksmith, will make any item to order.

Kentucky

FORT BOONSBOROUGH STATE PARK, Richmond, Kentucky 40475.

Cecil Orchard and Pat Allen make trammels, andirons, hooks, and all of the traditional wrought iron implements.

Charles Horrar (blacksmith), Valley View Forge, P.O. Box 41, Berea, Kentucky 40403.

Cranes, trivets, tools. Many items in stock, others to order.

WALLIN FORGE, Rt. 1, Box 65, Sparta, Kentucky 41086.

Toasting forks, cranes, pokers, fireplace tools, pot racks. Brochure available, $1.00

Maryland

CARROLL COUNTY FARM MUSEUM, 500 South Street, Westminster, Maryland 21157.

Employs both a working blacksmith and a tinsmith. Contact the blacksmith for further information and articles available: Randy McDaniels, 2501 East Mayberry Road, Silver Run, Maryland 21157.

Massachusetts

OLD STURBRIDGE VILLAGE, Rt. 20, Sturbridge, Massachusetts 01566.

Employs both tinsmiths and blacksmiths. A catalog describing the items they produce is available from the gift shop. A recent copy offered a tin reflector oven for roasting, andirons, and trivets, but more items than are shown are usually available or can be ordered.

SAUGUS IRON WORKS NATIONAL HISTORIC SITE, 244 Central Street, Saugus, Massachusetts 01906.

Two blacksmiths, Stephen Nichols and Bruce Dembling, produce items for open-hearth cooking. A catalogue available from the restoration shows some of these items. They include skewers, ladle and fork, and fireplace sets.

Charles A. Hartwell (tinsmith), 46 Hartwell Avenue, Littleton, Massachusetts 01460.

Complete line of nineteenth-century tinware. Price list available.

Newton Millham (blacksmith), 672 Drift Road, Westport, Massachusetts 02790.

Cranes, trammels, hooks, toasters, broilers, andirons, spits, spit jacks (clock jacks), ladles, forks, spatulas. Catalogue available, $1.00.

Michigan

FORT MACKINAC, Mackinac Island State Park Commission, Box 370, Mackinac Island, Michigan 49757.

The Benjamin Blacksmith Shop employs one blacksmith, Dennis Bradley. He produces a variety of fireplace cooking implements and accessories, including a fireplace shovel and poker (either plain or fancy), soup ladle, fork, spatula, fireplace toaster, and trammel hooks.

HENRY FORD MUSEUM AND GREENFIELD VILLAGE, Dearborn, Michigan 48121.

Employs two blacksmiths and a tinsmith. They produce a lengthy list of wares. Write to the merchandising department of the restoration for availability and prices.

Michael T. Machnik, 15586 Euclid, Allen Park, Michigan 48101.

Sixteenth-century through nineteenth-century reproductions of any implements and utensils.

Nebraska

STUHR MUSEUM–RAILROAD TOWN, 3133 W Hwy. 34, Grand Island, Nebraska 68801.

Ward Brinegar, their blacksmith, makes fireplace tools and other items to order.

FORT HARTSUFF STATE HISTORICAL PARK, Burwell, Nebraska 68823.

Employs two blacksmiths, Roger Frink and Ben Wados. They make lid-lifters, tongs, triangle supports, forks, and other items to order.

New Hampshire

STRAWBERRY BANKE, INC., P.O. Box 300, Portsmouth, New Hampshire 03801.

Peter Happny, their working blacksmith, will make items to order.

New Jersey

Jay Mickle (blacksmith), Headquarters Forge, Box 279, Stockton, New Jersey 08550.

Makes an inexpensive spit with skewers and brackets of contemporary design to the customer's specifications. Also, will make reproduction cooking andirons, cranes, pothooks, and other fireplace tools.

Frederick J. Rechsteiner (tinsmith), 1300 Buck Street, Millville, New Jersey 08332.

Reflecting ovens and reproductions of early American tinware.

L. Curtis Tindall, Jr. (blacksmith), 50 Everittstown Road, Frenchtown, New Jersey 08332.

Trivets, toasters, cranes, trammels, andirons, toasting forks, pot-hangers.

New York

THE FARMER'S MUSEUM, INC., Cooperstown, New York 13326.

Two blacksmiths, James Portues and David Jones, regularly make the more usual fireplace items, such as: hooks, forks, and fireplace sets; but they will make the more elaborate fireplace accessories to order.

MUSEUM VILLAGE IN ORANGE COUNTY, Monroe, New York 10950.

Employs two blacksmiths. Many items are available in the museum store, and most any other can be commissioned.

SLEEPY HOLLOW RESTORATIONS, Sales Department, 150 White Plains Road, Tarrytown, New York 10591.

Carries a tin reflector oven complete with iron spit and skewers.

WILLIAM SIDNEY MOUNT HOMESTEAD, The Museums at Stony Brook, Stony Brook, New York 11790.

Wrought iron items are available from the museum store. Write Ms. Linda Williams for a list and the prices.

Donald G. Carpentier (tinsmith), Box 145, R.D., East Nassau, New York 12062.

Reflector ovens, coffeepots, teapots, pans. Mr. Carpentier is also the founder of Eastfield Village and an active teacher of his craft there, as well.

Steve Kayne (blacksmith), 17 Harmon Place, Smithtown, New York 11787.

Cranes, toasters, skewers, trammels, S hooks, andirons, ladles, spoons, and spatulas. Catalogue available, $1.00.

North Carolina

OLD SALEM INC., Drawer F, Salem Station, Winston Salem, North Carolina 27108.
Employs two blacksmiths and three tinsmiths. Their items are available through the restoration's museum store.

David Brewin (blacksmith), John Campbell Folk School, Brasstown, North Carolina 28902.
Cranes, trammels, S hooks, ladles, forks, peels, broilers, spit hooks, spits, and andirons.

Ohio

HALE FARM AND VILLAGE, 2686 Oak Hill Road, Bath, Ohio 44210.
Barry Wheeler routinely makes pothooks and other simple implements for open-hearth cooking. Will do custom items on request.

OHIO VILLAGE, Ohio Historical Society, 1982 Velma Avenue, Columbus, Ohio 43211.
Three resident craftsmen, a blacksmith and two tinsmiths, will make on demand a variety of fireplace cooking implements including fireplace tools, S hooks, andirons, and tin kitchens for both baking and roasting.

Mark Bokenkamp (blacksmith), Bokenkamp's Forge, 10132 Liberty Road, Powell, Ohio 43065.
Andirons, cranes, trammels, fireplace tools, cooking utensils, S hooks, and spits.

Pennsylvania

HISTORIC SCHAEFFERSTOWN, Schaefferstown, Pennsylvania 17088.
Employs two tinsmiths, Lee Troxel and Charles Merkel, and one blacksmith, Richard McCune. All three craftsmen produce many items, mostly on special order.

MEADOWCROFT VILLAGE, R.D. #2, Avella, Pennsylvania 15312.
Glenn Kline, their blacksmith, will make most fireplace items to order.

PENNSYLVANIA FARM MUSEUM, 2451 Kissel Hill Road, Lancaster, Pennsylvania 17601.
A blacksmith and a tinsmith make various items which are sold through the museum's gift shop.

Thomas Loose (blacksmith), Rt. 2, Box 124, Leesport, Pennsylvania 19533.

Cranes, trammels, trivets, toasters, andirons with spit, spiders, skewers, forks, ladles, spatulas. Brochure available.

Oregon

PIONEER VILLAGE, P.O. Box 237, 725 North 5th, Jacksonville, Oregon 97530.

Jim Converse, their blacksmith, will make all types of open-hearth cooking accessories.

Utah

OLD DESERET PIONEER VILLAGE, Pioneer Trail State Park, 2601 Sunnyside Avenue, Salt Lake City, Utah 84108.

Russ Martin, their blacksmith, can make most any item in wrought iron including cranes, andirons, shovels, peels, trivets, skewers, etc., to order.

Vermont

Robert Bourdon (blacksmith), Wolcott, Vermont 05680.

Pot-lifters, shovels, tongs, cranes, trammels, andirons, trivets, toasters, salamanders, frying pans, skimmers, toasting forks, ladles, meat forks, skewers.

Pete Taggett (blacksmith), The Blacksmith Shop, Inc., Box 15, Mount Holly, Vermont 05758.

Cranes, S hooks, trammels, spits, andirons. Catalogue available, $1.00.

TWANKY DILLO FORGE, Ian Eddy and Leigh Morrell (blacksmiths), R.F.D. 1, Box 213, Putney, Vermont 05346.

Hand-wrought iron items including cranes, trammels, S hooks, andirons, trivets, spits. Custom work to order.

Virginia

COLONIAL WILLIAMSBURG, Williamsburg, Virginia 23185.

Employs three working blacksmiths who sell their work in two stores at the restoration (Tarpley's and Prentis') and through a direct mail catalog available from: Colonial Williamsburg, 201 5th Ave., Box CH, Williamsburg, Virginia 23185. Recent catalogues have included a revolving toaster, wafer iron, trivet, and fireplace tools.

John A. Careatti (tinsmith and blacksmith), Rt. #1, Box 154, Howertons, Virginia 22475.

Reflector ovens, spoons, dippers, salamanders, trivets, shovels, toasters, etc.

Making Your Hearth Implements

For the inveterate do-it-yourselfer, here is a list of issues of *Early American Life* magazine that includes articles on making your own hearth cooking equipment. Published by the Early American Society, *Early American Life* is a popular magazine devoted to the understanding of American social history and modern interpretations of its early arts, crafts, furnishings, and architecture. Back issues of the magazine can be borrowed from public libraries that subscribe to *Early American Life*. Two of these articles—making a tin kitchen and a fireplace trivet—have been reprinted in *The Early American Fireplace Book*, recently published by the Society.

"Forging A Fireplace Toaster," *Early American Life*, February, 1980.
"Forging A Fireplace Trivet," *Early American Life*, April, 1979.
"Plans for A Tin Kitchen," *Early American Life*, October, 1976.

And if you are really starting from scratch, two books, *The Forgotten Art of Building and Using A Brick Bake Oven*, by Richard M. Bacon, and *The Forgotten Art of Building A Good Fireplace*, by Vrest Orton, will be invaluable. Both are available from Yankee Books. To order them, write: Book Department, Box F, Yankee, Inc., Depot Square, Peterborough, New Hampshire 03458.

Selected Bibliography

ANDERSON, JEAN. *Recipes From America's Restored Villages.* Garden City, New York: Doubleday & Company, Inc., 1975.*

ARESTY, ESTHER B. *The Delectable Past.* New York: Simon and Schuster, 1964.

BACON, RICHARD M. *The Forgotten Arts.* Dublin, New Hampshire: Yankee, Inc., 1978.

——————. *The Forgotten Art of Building and Using a Brick Bake Oven.* Dublin, New Hampshire: Yankee, Inc., 1977.

BELOTE, JULIANNE, *The Compleat American Housewife 1776.* Concord, California: Nitty Gritty Productions, 1974.*

BOORSTIN, DANIEL J. *The Americans: The Colonial Experience.* New York: Random House, 1958.

BOOTH, LETHA and THE STAFF OF COLONIAL WILLIAMSBURG, compilers. *The Williamsburg Cookbook.* Williamsburg, Virginia: The Colonial Williamsburg Foundation, 1971.*

Boston Cookbook of 1883 (excerpts from), Wakefield, Massachusetts: Pride Publications, Inc., 1979.

BRADLEY, MARTHA. *The British Housewife.* London, c. 1770.

BROOME COUNTY HISTORICAL SOCIETY. *The American Hearth, Colonial and Post-Colonial Cooking Tools.* Binghamton, New York: Roberson Center for the Arts and Sciences, 1976.

BULLOCK, HELEN. *The Williamsburg Art of Cookery.* Williamsburg, Virginia: The Colonial Williamsburg Foundation, 1939.*

CARSON, JANE. *Colonial Virginia Cookery*. Williamsburg, Virginia: The Colonial Williamsburg Foundation, 1968.

CARTER, SUSANNAH. *The Frugal Colonial Housewife*. Edited and illustrated by Jean McKibbin. Garden City, Long Island: Dolphin Books, Doubleday and Company, Inc.

CLUSELLS, SYLVAIN. *Cooking on Turning Spit & Grill*. Translated by Charles R. Liebman. London: Arthur Barker Limited, 1961.

COSENTINO, GERALDINE, and REGINA STEWART. *Kitchenware, A Golden Handbook of Collectibles*. New York: Golden Press, 1977.

DEMOS, JOHN. *A Little Commonwealth, Family Life in Plymouth Colony*. New York: Oxford University Press, 1970.

DONOVAN, MARY, AMY HATRAK, FRANCES MILLS, and ELIZABETH SHULL. *The Thirteen Colonies Cookbook*. New York: Praeger Publishers, Inc., 1975.*

EARLE, ALICE MORSE. *Home Life in Colonial Days*. New York: The Macmillan Company, 1898.

ELVERSON, VIRGINIA T., and MARY McLANAHAN. *A Cooking Legacy*. New York: Cornerstone Library, 1976.*

FARRINGTON, DORIS E. *Fireside Cooks & Black Kettle Recipes*. Indianapolis and New York: The Bobbs–Merrill Company, 1976.*

FEARS, J. WAYNE. *Backcountry Cooking*. Charlotte, North Carolina: Fast & Macmillan Publishers, Inc., 1980.

Food, Drink, and Recipes of Early New England. Sturbridge, Massachusetts: Old Sturbridge Village Booklet Series, 1963.*

FRANKLIN, LINDA CAMPBELL. *From Hearth to Cookstove*. Orlando, Florida: The House of Collectibles, Inc., 1978.

GLASSE, HANNAH. *The Art of Cookery Made Plain and Easy* (reprint of 1796 edition). Hamden, Connecticut: Archon Books, 1971.

GROW, LAWRENCE, ed. *The Second Old House Catalogue*. New York: Universe Books, 1978.

HAAS, IRVIN. *America's Historic Villages & Restorations*. New York: Arco Publishing Company, Inc., 1974.

HALVERSON, DEBORAH G., ed. *The Early American Life Fireplace Book*. Harrisburg, Pennsylvania: The Early American Society, 1980.

HARRIS, HESTER. *Cast Iron Cookbook*. Concord, California: Nitty Gritty Productions, 1969.

HARRISON, MOLLY. *The Kitchen In History.* New York: Charles Scribner's Sons, 1972.

HECHTLINGER, ADELAIDE. *The Seasonal Hearth, The Woman At Home In Early America.* Woodstock, New York: The Overlook Press, 1977.

HOLM, DON. *The Old-Fashioned Dutch Oven Cookbook.* Caldwell, Idaho: The Caxton Printers, Ltd., 1976.

JONES, EVAN. *American Food: The Gastronomic Story* (second edition). New York: Random House & Vintage Books, 1981.*

KAUFFMAN, HENRY J. *Early American Ironware, Cast and Wrought.* New York: Weathervane Books, 1966.

KAUFFMAN, HENRY J., and QUENTIN H. BOWERS. *Early American Andirons and Other Fireplace Accessories.* Nashville: Thomas Nelson, Inc., 1974.

LANTZ, LOUISE K. *Old American Kitchenware 1725–1925.* Nashville: Thomas Nelson, Inc.; and Hanover, Pennsylvania: Everybodys Press, 1970.

LARK, DAVID. "Early American Kitchens," *Gourmet* (November 1969), pp. 17–19, 47–52.

LESLIE, ELIZA. *Directions for Cookery in its Various Branches* (reprint of 1848 edition). New York: The Arno Press Inc., 1973.

LECOQ, RAYMOND. *Les Objets de la Vie Domestique.* Paris: Berger–Levrault, 1979.

LYON, J. C. *The Fireplace Cook Book.* Santa Fe: Lightning Tree, 1975.

ORTON, VREST. *The Forgotten Art of Building a Good Fireplace.* Dublin, New Hampshire: Yankee, Inc., 1974.

PHIPPS, FRANCES. *Colonial Kitchens, Their Furnishings and Their Gardens.* New York: Hawthorn Books, Inc., 1972.

ROBERSON, JOHN and MARIE. *The Complete Barbecue Cookbook.* New York: Collier Books, 1967.

ROOT, WAVERLY, and RICHARD DE ROCHEMONT. *Eating in America, A History.* New York: William Morrow & Company, Inc., 1976.

RAGSDALE, JOHN G. *Dutch Oven Cooking.* Houston: Pacesetter Press, 1973.

RANDOLPH, MARY. *The Virginia Housewife.* Philadelphia, 1855.

Restored Village Directory. 5th ed. New York: Quadrant Press, Inc., 1978.

ROWSOME, FRANK, JR. *The Bright and Glowing Place.* Brattleboro, Vermont: The Stephen Greene Press, 1975.

SZATHMÁRY, LOUIS. *American Gastronomy*. Chicago: Henry Regnery Company, 1974.*

SIMMONS, AMELIA. *American Cookery* (reprint of 1796 edition). Harriman, Tennessee: Pioneer Press, 1976.

TANNAHILL, REAY. *Food In History*. New York: Stein & Day, 1973.

  * These volumes have been selected for the readers who wish to prepare an authentic early American feast in their fireplace. All of the books indicated contain either recipes or menus, or both, from primary sources which have already been tested and adjusted to fit twentieth-century ingredients and measurements. Directions for preparing them with gas and electric appliances are also normally included. Most of these books can be readily found in a public library.

  Also included in this list is *American Gastronomy*, by Louis Szathmáry, which may be a little more difficult to locate on your local library shelves. It is well worth the search, though, if you are eager to try original recipes from some of the early cookbooks also included in this bibliography, now available in reprint editions, or recipes from other primary sources. Mr. Szathmáry, a professional chef, restaurateur, and collector of rare cookbooks, devotes a whole chapter here to his excellent observations on how to translate antique recipes for use today. So, if you're ever confronted with a recipe which directs you to add one wine glass of sherry, or a gill of brandy to the cake batter, this is the place to begin!

Index